The Wild Side

ANGRY ANIMALS

The Wild Side

ANGRY ANIMALS

Henry Billings
Melissa Billings

JAMESTOWN  PUBLISHERS

a division of NTC/CONTEMPORARY PUBLISHING GROUP
Lincolnwood, Illinois USA

ISBN 0–8092-9516-4

Published by Jamestown Publishers,
a division of NTC/Contemporary Publishing Group, Inc.
4255 West Touhy Avenue,
Lincolnwood (Chicago), Illinois 60712-1975, U.S.A.

00 01 02 03 04 VL 10 9 8 7 6 5 4 3 2 1

CONTENTS

UNIT THREE

To the Student

From the time we can barely walk or talk, we feel a kinship with animals. Toddlers are excited when they see a cat, a puppy, a horse, or a duck. They may reach out to touch the animal but pull back in fear when it makes a quick or unexpected move. We instinctively feel a connection with animals but understand that animals are different from us in a variety of ways.

The articles in this book spotlight the awesome powers of animals, powers that are unleashed when animals are angry or frightened or simply acting from instinct. These articles are not meant to make you fearful of animals. Instead, they serve as a reminder that animals must be respected. They prove to us that we share our world with creatures that can be ruthless, combative, persistent, intelligent, cunning, unpredictable, and altogether fascinating.

As you read and enjoy the 15 articles in this book, you will be developing your reading skills. If you complete all the lessons in this book, you will surely increase your reading speed and improve your reading comprehension and critical thinking skills. Also, because these exercises include items of the types often found on state and national tests, learning how to complete them will prepare you for tests you may have to take in the future.

How to Use This Book

About the Book.   *Angry Animals* contains three units, each of which includes five lessons. Each lesson begins with an article about an unusual subject or event. The article is followed by a group of four reading comprehension exercises and three critical thinking exercises. The reading comprehension exercises will help you understand the article. The critical thinking exercises will help you think about what you have read and how it relates to your own experience.

At the end of each lesson, you will also have the opportunity to give your personal response to some aspect of the article and then to assess how well you understood what you read.

The Sample Lesson.   Working through the sample lesson, the first lesson in the book, with your class or group will demonstrate how a lesson is organized. The sample lesson explains how to complete the exercises and score your answers. The correct answers for the sample exercises and sample scores are printed in lighter type. In some cases, explanations of the correct answers are given. The explanations will help you understand how to think through these question types.

If you have any questions about how to complete the exercises or score them, this is the time to get the answers.

Working Through Each Lesson.   Begin each lesson by looking at the photograph and reading the caption. Before you read, predict what you think the article will be about. Then read the article.

Sometimes your teacher may decide to time your reading. Timing helps you keep track of and increase your reading speed. If you have been timed, enter your reading time in the box at the end of the lesson. Then use the Words-per-Minute Table to find your reading speed, and record your speed on the Reading Speed graph at the end of the unit.

Next complete the Reading Comprehension and Critical Thinking exercises. The directions for each exercise will tell you how to mark your answers. When you have finished all four Reading Comprehension exercises, use the answer key provided by your teacher to check your work. Follow the directions after each exercise to find your score. Record your Reading Comprehension scores on the graph at the end of each unit. Then check your answers to the Author's Approach, Summarizing and Paraphrasing, and Critical Thinking exercises. Fill in the Critical Thinking Chart at the end of each unit with your evaluation of your work and comments about your progress.

At the end of each unit you will also complete a Compare and Contrast Chart. The completed chart will help you see what the articles have in common, and it will give you an opportunity to explore your own ideas about the events in the articles.

SAMPLE
LESSON

The Menace of Pit Bulls

Betty Lou Stidham lived in terror. She feared the dogs next door to her—two ferocious pit bulls. Earlier, these dogs had mauled Stidham's own dog. Stidham, who lived alone, asked the city to have the two pit bulls put to sleep. But officials in Memphis, Tennessee, said no. They said her dog had caused the attack. It had stuck its paw through the neighbor's fence.

2   And so, on a steamy day in 1990, Betty Lou Stidham walked out to her mailbox to get the mail. As she walked back toward her house, the two pit bulls struck. Somehow they had gotten outside their chain-link fence. Fifty-seven-year-old Stidham never had a chance. The snarling dogs jumped all over her. Karen Gomez was driving by in her car at the time. "There was this large body [Stidham weighed 200 pounds] with hardly any clothes on," said Gomez. "There was a dog on each side pulling on the body, which seemed lifeless."

3   But Stidham wasn't dead—not yet. She did what she could to fend off the pit bulls. A neighbor who witnessed part of the struggle said, "At times [Stidham] would raise her right hand up. When she did, [the dogs] would attack the hand. You could tell she was still alive, maybe barely."

4   The neighbor desperately wanted to help Stidham. Grabbing two brooms, she began to run toward the dogs. But a friend stopped her. "She beat on me with her fists to let her go help," said the friend. "But I couldn't let her do it. They would have killed her too." Meanwhile, someone had called 911. An ambulance arrived and rushed Stidham to the hospital. But it was too late. Stidham had lost too much blood. She died four hours later.

5   Betty Lou Stidham isn't the only person to be attacked by angry pit bulls. In Michigan, a pit bull broke out of its owner's backyard. It went into a neighbor's yard where young Kyle Corullo was playing. The pit bull killed the little boy by breaking his neck. In Alabama, two pit bulls attacked Johnny Ford as he jogged. Ford, who was the city's mayor, saved himself by climbing up a tree. Still, the dogs did plenty of damage. They nearly ripped off one of Ford's legs.

6   Dozens of people have been mauled or killed by pit bulls in recent years. What makes these dogs so vicious? Pit bulls—which are really bull terriers—are strongly built. And they have been bred to be fierce. It has been said that a pit bull would rather fight than eat. In the 1800s, some owners set up fights between these dogs. Two dogs would be put into a pit. They would fight while people, who bet on one dog or the other, cheered.

7   Although pit bull fighting is now against the law, some people still use the dogs as fighters. Some use the

The pit bull has been bred for hundreds of years to be a fearless fighter. But now, especially in urban areas, many people feel that this guard dog is too ferocious for its own good.

dogs for protection. They keep pit bulls as guard dogs. Others just like the breed. They say that a well-trained pit bull can make a marvelous pet. They are loyal and they love to be around people. "There's no dog that has a bigger heart," said one pit bull owner. "You can just feel the love coming from this dog."

8   In fact, many dog experts claim that the problem lies not with the dogs but with the owners. Some people treat their pit bulls badly. Others don't bother to train the dogs properly. So perhaps the owners are to blame for pit bull attacks. Today, owners in some places face fines or even jail if their pit bulls attack someone.

9   So, is the pit bull a good dog or a bad dog? It depends. If the dog is curled up on your lap by the fire, it's a good dog. But if it's tearing at your arm, it's a real menace.

If you have been timed while reading this article, enter your reading time below. Then turn to the Words-per-Minute Table on page 55 and look up your reading speed (words per minute). Enter your reading speed on the graph on page 56.

Reading Time: Sample Lesson

_____ : _____
Minutes   Seconds

A | Finding the Main Idea

One statement below expresses the main idea of the article. One statement is too general, or too broad. The other statement explains only part of the article; it is too narrow. Label the statements using the following key:

M—Main Idea   B—Too Broad   N—Too Narrow

__B__   1. Some dogs can be very dangerous and should not be trusted. [This statement is too broad. The article is about a particular kind of dog, the pit bull.]

__M__   2. Bred to be fighters, pit bulls can be vicious pets. [This is the main idea. It tells what the article is about—the pit bull. It also tells you what the dog is like.]

__N__   3. In the 1800s some owners set up fights between pit bulls and bet on which would win. [This statement is true, but it is too narrow. It gives only one piece, or detail, from the article.]

__15__	Score 15 points for a correct M answer.
__10__	Score 5 points for each correct B or N answer.
__25__	**Total Score:** Finding the Main Idea

B | Recalling Facts

How well do you remember the facts in the article? Put an X in the box next to the answer that correctly completes each statement about the article.

1. Betty Lou Stidham feared the dogs next door because
- ☐ a. they made too much noise.
- ☒ b. they had hurt her dog.
- ☐ c. she disliked all dogs.

2. A pit bull killed young Kyle Corullo by
- ☒ a. breaking his neck.
- ☐ b. tearing an artery.
- ☐ c. cutting off his air supply.

3. Betty Stidham was attacked by pit bulls while
- ☐ a. sitting in her living room.
- ☐ b. teasing the dogs.
- ☒ c. walking back from her mailbox.

4. Pit bulls are really a kind of
- ☒ a. collie.
- ☐ b. terrier.
- ☐ c. spaniel.

5. A pit bull can be a good dog if it is
- ☐ a. trained properly.
- ☒ b. always kept away from people.
- ☐ c. ignored all the time.

Score 5 points for each correct answer.	
__25__	**Total Score:** Recalling Facts

C | Making Inferences

When you combine your own experience with information from a text to draw a conclusion that is not directly stated in that text, you are making an inference. Below are five statements that may or may not be inferences based on information in the article. Label the statements using the following key:

C—Correct Inference   F—Faulty Inference

___F___ 1. You can always count on a strong chain-link fence to keep pit bulls away from you. [This is a faulty inference. The pit bulls next door to Betty Stidham found a way out of their fenced yard.]

___C___ 2. More than other dog owners, pit bull owners have a responsibility to care for their pets. [This is a correct inference. Since pit bulls have been bred to be fighters, it is especially important to train and treat them properly.]

___F___ 3. Once a pit bull has pulled its victim down to the ground, it loses interest in him or her. [This is a faulty inference. The pit bulls continued to attack Betty Stidham even after she was down.]

___C___ 4. In the hands of cruel or violent people, the pit bull could be a dangerous weapon. [This is a correct inference. It would be easy, it seems, to train a pit bull to be as violent as its owner wishes.]

___C___ 5. Pit bulls cannot climb trees. [This is a correct inference. Mayor Johnny Ford escaped from a pit bull by climbing a tree.]

Score 5 points for each correct answer.

___25___ **Total Score:** Making Inferences

D | Using Words Precisely

Each numbered sentence below contains an underlined word or phrase from the article. Following the sentence are three definitions. One definition is closest to the meaning of the underlined word. One definition is opposite or nearly opposite. Label those two definitions using the following key; do not label the remaining definition.

C—Closest   O—Opposite or Nearly Opposite

1. She feared the dogs next door to her—two <u>ferocious</u> pit bulls.
___O___ a. friendly and gentle
___C___ b. fierce; brutal
_____ c. young

2. Earlier, these dogs had <u>mauled</u> Stidham's own dog.
___C___ a. injured
___O___ b. come to the aid of
_____ c. passed by

3. She did what she could to <u>fend off</u> the pit bulls.
___O___ a. invite to come closer
_____ b. remember
___C___ c. drive away

4. What makes these dogs so <u>vicious</u>?
_____ a. unusual
___O___ b. peaceful; kind
___C___ c. savage; violent

5. But if it's tearing at your arm, it's a real <u>menace</u>.

_____C_____ a. one who threatens to harm others

_____ b. shock

_____O_____ c. one who tries to help others

_____15_____ Score 3 points for each correct C answer.

_____10_____ Score 2 points for each correct O answer.

_____25_____ **Total Score:** Using Words Precisely

Enter the four total scores in the spaces below, and add them together to find your Reading Comprehension Score. Then record your score on the graph on page 57.

Score	Question Type	Sample Lesson
25	Finding the Main Idea	
25	Recalling Facts	
25	Making Inferences	
25	Using Words Precisely	
100	**Reading Comprehension Score**	

Author's Approach

Put an X in the box next to the correct answer.

1. The authors use the first sentence of the article to

☒ a. make the reader curious about what was frightening Betty Lou Stidham.

☐ b. describe Betty Lou Stidham's personality.

☐ c. compare pit bulls and other dogs.

2. From the statements below, choose those that you believe the authors would agree with.

☐ a. No one should be allowed to own pit bulls, since these dogs are so vicious.

☒ b. Pit bulls need to be treated with kindness, or they may become vicious.

☐ c. People who are afraid of pit bulls are foolish.

3. What is the authors' purpose in writing "The Menace of Pit Bulls"?

☐ a. to persuade readers not to own pit bulls

☒ b. to inform readers about how vicious some pit bulls may be

☐ c. to describe the way some owners feel about their pit bulls

4. Choose the statement below that best describes the authors' position in paragraph 7.

☒ a. Different people have different reasons for keeping pit bulls.

☐ b. Using pit bulls as guard dogs makes them dangerous.

☐ c. No dog is more gentle and loving than the pit bull.

_____4_____ Number of correct answers

Record your personal assessment of your work on the Critical Thinking Chart on page 58.

Summarizing and Paraphrasing

Put an X in the box next to the correct answer.

1. Below are summaries of the article. Choose the summary that says all the most important things about the article but in the fewest words.

☐ a. Pit bulls can be dangerous. [This summary leaves out almost all of the important details, such as how and why pit bulls are dangerous.]

☐ b. Pit bulls may attack no reason at all, as one attacked Betty Lou Stidham in her . Many people agree that because pit bulls were bred to be fighters in the 1800s they are too dangerous to be kept as pets, even if some people claim that they are loyal and lovable. [This summary presents important ideas from the article but includes too many unnecessary details.]

☒ c. Although some people love pit bulls, these dogs can be unpredictable and vicious. [This summary says all the most important things about the article in the fewest words.]

2. Read the statement from the article below. Then read the paraphrase of that statement. Choose the reason that best tells why the paraphrase does not say the same thing as the statement.

   Statement: It has been said that a pit bull would rather fight than eat.

   Paraphrase: Pit bulls do not enjoy fighting, nor do they like to eat.

☐ a. Paraphrase says too much.

☐ b. Paraphrase doesn't say enough.

☒ c. Paraphrase doesn't agree with the statement. [The first statement implies that pit bulls enjoy fighting so much that they would choose to fight over an enjoyable activity such as eating. The second statement says that pit bulls don't enjoy either fighting or eating.]

__3__ Number of correct answers

Record your personal assessment of your work on the Critical Thinking Chart on page 58.

Critical Thinking

Follow the directions provided for questions 1, 2, and 3. Put an X in the box next to the correct answer for the other questions.

1. For each statement below, write O if it expresses an opinion or write F if it expresses a fact.

   __F__ a. Pit bulls are stronger than many other dogs.

   __O__ b. You can never trust a pit bull.

   __O__ c. Only people who don't care about their neighbors would own a pit bull.

2. Choose from the letters below to correctly complete the following statement. Write the letters on the lines.

   On the positive side, _b_ , but on the negative side _c_ .

   a. some people use pit bulls as guard dogs

   b. pit bulls can be brave and loyal

   c. pit bulls can be vicious and mean

3. Reread paragraph 6. Then choose from the letters below to correctly complete the following statement. Write the letters on the lines.

   According to paragraph 6, ___c___ because ___a___.

   a. in the past, pit bulls were bred to be fighters

   b. pit bulls are really bull terriers

   c. today's pit bulls are sometimes vicious

4. If you were a dog trainer, how could you use the information in the article to train pit bulls?

   ☐ a. Be nervous and afraid around pit bulls because they can become dangerous.

   ☒ b. Know that you need to take special care in training pit bulls or they could become dangerous.

   ☐ c. Refuse to train pit bulls because these dogs are dangerous.

5. What did you have to do to answer question 3?

   ☒ a. find a cause (why something happened)

   ☐ b. find an opinion (what someone thinks about something)

   ☐ c. make a prediction (what might happen next)

   ___5___ Number of correct answers

   Record your personal assessment of your work on the Critical Thinking Chart on page 58.

Personal Response

A question I would like answered by Johnny Ford is _____

___[Write a question to ask Johnny Ford concerning his brush___

___with death when the pit bull attacked him.]___

_____

_____

Self-Assessment

Before reading this article, I already knew _____

___[Recall facts you knew about pit bull attacks or attacks by___

___other vicious dogs.]___

_____

_____

_____

Self-Assessment

To get the most out of the *Wild Side* series, you need to take charge of your own progress in improving your reading comprehension and critical thinking skills. Here are some of the features that help you work on those essential skills.

Reading Comprehension Exercises. Complete these exercises immediately after reading each article. They help you recall what you have read, understand the stated and implied main ideas, and add words to your working vocabulary.

Critical Thinking Skills Exercises. These exercises help you focus on the authors' approach and purpose, recognize and generate summaries and paraphrases, and identify relationships between ideas.

Personal Response and Self-Assessment. Questions in this category help you relate the articles to your personal experience and give you the opportunity to evaluate your understanding of the information in that lesson.

Compare and Contrast Charts. At the end of each unit you will complete a Compare and Contrast Chart. The completed chart helps you see what the articles have in common and gives you an opportunity to explore your own ideas about the topics discussed in the articles.

The Graphs. The graphs and charts at the end of each unit enable you to keep track of your progress. Check your graphs regularly with your teacher. Decide whether your progress is satisfactory or whether you need additional work on some skills. What types of exercises are you having difficulty with? Talk with your teacher about ways to work on the skills in which you need the most practice.

UNIT ONE

A Whale of a Tale

On August 12, 1819, a whaling ship called the *Essex* sailed from New England. On board were 20 men. They were whalers, men who killed whales for their valuable oil. The men planned to be at sea for two and a half years. In the first 15 months, things went smoothly. The whalers found and killed 25 whales. But on November 20, 1820, everything changed. On that day, a whale fought back. Suddenly, the hunters became the hunted.

2 The crew of the *Essex* was used to working in dangerous conditions.

Nineteenth-century whalers hunted whales for their oil, bones, and meat. Hunting huge whales in small, unprotected boats was a risky way to make a living.

After all, they could not do their job from the deck of the main ship. If they could have, the job would have been a lot easier. The *Essex* was a sturdy 238 tons. Instead, the men had to get right next to the whales. They needed to get close enough to plunge their harpoons into the creatures' sides. So they had to leave the *Essex* and do their hunting in small whaleboats. These boats were just 28 feet long and 6 feet wide. They didn't weigh much, either. They were made from planks of wood that were less than half an inch thick.

3   In these small boats, the men went after giant sperm whales. An adult sperm whale might measure well over 80 feet—almost the length of the *Essex* itself. Its tail could be 20 feet wide. If a whale's tail ever hit one of the fragile whaleboats, it would smash it to bits. So the men had to maneuver their boats with great care. On November 20, the *Essex* was far out in the Pacific Ocean. In the early morning the men spotted whales. Two men stayed on the *Essex* while the others climbed into three whaleboats. Each boat carried six men. George Pollard, the captain, commanded one boat. Owen Chase,

the first mate, sailed in the second boat. Matthew Joy, the second mate, led the third boat.

4   The whalers rowed far from the *Essex*. They drew closer and closer to the group of sperm whales. Finally, Chase's crew drew alongside one. Chase stood at the bow and plunged his harpoon into the whale. The whale flipped its tail, grazing the boat. The blow was enough to punch a hole in the side of the light boat.

5   Chase knew his men could not continue with the hunt. The other two whaleboats would have to go on alone. Chase cut the line to his harpoon. Then he stuffed the crew's jackets into the gaping hole in the boat. Chase told one man to bail out the water. He ordered the others to row back to the *Essex* as fast as they could.

6   When they returned to the *Essex*, Chase began to repair the whaleboat with a piece of canvas. Suddenly, he saw a sperm whale. It was huge. Chase guessed that it was 85 feet long. The creature was just 100 yards away. Yet Chase was not worried. Whales are not vicious. In fact, most of the time they are rather playful.

7   There was nothing playful about this whale, however. It spouted two or three times then disappeared below the surface. When it came up again, it was only 30 yards away. The whale was moving straight at the *Essex*. Chase couldn't believe his eyes. He ordered one of his men to steer the *Essex* out of the way. But it was too late. The giant whale rammed into the ship with its massive 20-foot head. The blow knocked the men to their knees. They all looked at each other in amazement. No one spoke. No one knew what to say. They had never heard of a whale attacking a ship before. And this whale wasn't finished. After hitting the ship, the whale swam under it. Moments later, it came up on the other side. It appeared dazed. It thrashed about, opening and snapping its huge jaws. Then one of the men shouted, "Here he is—he is making for us again."

8   It didn't seem possible. But the whale was attacking the *Essex* a second time. It charged at the ship with twice the speed of the first attack. It lifted its blunt head half out of the water. Foamy waves kicked up on both sides as the whale gained speed and fury.

9   This time the whale hit the ship with such force that it crushed the bow. Chase knew the *Essex* was doomed. He told his men to jump into a whaleboat. In a few moments, they rowed safely away. The men watched silently as the ship tipped over on its side.

10   For the whale, the story ends there. The creature was never seen again. But for the men of the *Essex*, the story was just beginning. When the two other whaleboats returned from the hunt, the men were stunned to find the *Essex* lying on its side. The whalers got back on the ship for a brief time. They grabbed some sails. They also rescued some biscuits, water, a few guns, tools, and nails.

11   But the men faced a grim future. They were stuck in three tiny boats in the middle of the ocean. The nearest land was thousands of miles away. It didn't seem likely that they would reach land before they ran out of food and water.

12   That first day, no one ate. The men had no appetite. Some of them cried. Only a few were able to sleep that night. Most just stared at the black water, wondering what would become of them.

13   Days passed. Sometimes the wind blew the boats along at a good pace. Other times, there was no breeze at all. Then the boats just bobbed up and down in the water. The hot sun beat down without mercy. It was tough on the men. Some began to lose their will to live. Then, on December 20, one of the men stood up and shouted, "There is land!"

14   By a stroke of pure luck, the three boats had drifted toward a tiny island. The island wasn't on any map. Today it is known as Henderson's Island.

15   When the men saw the land, their hopes surged. They were saved! But they weren't. The island had fresh water, but almost no food. There wasn't nearly enough to keep 20 men alive. So, after a week, Pollard told the men they would be better off getting back into the whaleboats. Three men refused. They vowed to take their chances staying on the island.

16   These three men were lucky. They were later rescued. But the 17 who sailed off were not so fortunate. They drifted for nearly two more months. Some of the men died of hunger. To survive, the others ate the flesh of those who died.

17   In time, the wind blew the three boats far away from each other. One was never seen again. On February 17, 1821, a passing ship spotted one of the whaleboats. It contained Chase and two other men. Six days later, a different ship rescued Pollard and one other from the third whaleboat. These survivors had been in their tiny boats for three months and had sailed 3,000 miles.

18   In all, only eight members of the crew survived. Twelve died at sea. The sad story of the *Essex* did have one bright spot, however. It inspired one of the great novels of all time. After learning about the whale's bizarre attack, author Herman Melville wrote a similar story in his classic book, *Moby Dick*.

A Finding the Main Idea

One statement below expresses the main idea of the article. One statement is too general, or too broad. The other statement explains only part of the article; it is too narrow. Label the statements using the following key:

M—Main Idea   **B—Too Broad**   **N—Too Narrow**

_____ B   1. The whale that attacked the *Essex*, a whaling ship from New England, was estimated to be about 85 feet long.

_____ M   2. During the *Essex*'s tragic whaling trip in 1820, a whale attack set off a chain of events that ended in the death of 12 whalers

_____ N   3. A rare whale attack caused the death of a group of whalers.

_____ Score 15 points for a correct M answer.

_____ Score 5 points for each correct B or N answer.

_____ **Total Score:** Finding the Main Idea

B Recalling Facts

How well do you remember the facts in the article? Put an X in the box next to the answer that correctly completes each statement about the article.

1. Whalers usually hunted whales from
   - ☐ a. small but sturdy rafts.
   - ☒ b. small whaleboats only about 28 feet long.
   - ☐ c. the deck of their main ship.

2. Chase's group was forced to give up the hunt when
   - ☐ a. Chase lost his harpoon in the whale's tail.
   - ☐ b. the whale attacked the *Essex* and they had to turn back to protect the main ship.
   - ☒ c. the whale's tail punched a hole in the whaleboat.

3. Just after the whale attacked the *Essex*, most of the crew
   - ☒ a. were amazed.
   - ☐ b. felt angry.
   - ☐ c. were badly injured.

4. Many of the crew decided not to stay on Henderson's Island because it
   - ☐ a. had no fresh water.
   - ☐ b. was too hot.
   - ☒ c. had almost no food.

5. The survivors who stayed with their whaleboats were rescued after three
   - ☐ a. weeks at sea.
   - ☒ b. months at sea.
   - ☐ c. years at sea.

Score 5 points for each correct answer.

_____ **Total Score:** Recalling Facts

C Making Inferences

When you combine your own experience with information from a text to draw a conclusion that is not directly stated in that text, you are making an inference. Below are five statements that may or may not be inferences based on information in the article. Label the statements using the following key:

C—Correct Inference   **F—Faulty Inference**

__C__ 1. Whales are usually very easy to hunt.

__C__ 2. The surviving crew members had interesting tales to tell about their adventures.

__F__ 3. The whale never meant to hurt the ship; it ran into the *Essex* by mistake.

__F__ 4. There wasn't much room for food and supplies on the three whaleboats.

__F__ 5. All the men would definitely have survived if they had stayed on the island.

Score 5 points for each correct answer.

_____ **Total Score:** Making Inferences

D Using Words Precisely

Each numbered sentence below contains an underlined word or phrase from the article. Following the sentence are three definitions. One definition is closest to the meaning of the underlined word. One definition is opposite or nearly opposite. Label those two definitions using the following key; do not label the remaining definition.

C—Closest   **O—Opposite or Nearly Opposite**

1. They were whalers, men who killed whales for their <u>valuable</u> oil.

__C__ a. precious

__O__ b. worthless

_____ c. fragrant

2. Moments later, the whale came up on the other side. It appeared <u>dazed</u>.

__O__ a. alert

_____ b. old

__C__ c. confused

3. Chase knew the *Essex* was <u>doomed.</u>

_____ a. likely to need repairs

__C__ b. unlikely to recover from the damage

__O__ c. sure to survive the attack

4. They <u>vowed</u> to take their chances staying on the island.

__O__ a. refused

__C__ b. promised

_____ c. hoped

5. But the 17 who sailed off were not so <u>fortunate</u>.

_____ a. lucky

_____ b. intelligent

_____ c. unlucky

_____ Score 3 points for each correct C answer.

_____ Score 2 points for each correct O answer.

_____ **Total Score:** Using Words Precisely

Enter the four total scores in the spaces below, and add them together to find your Reading Comprehension Score. Then record your score on the graph on page 57.

Score	Question Type	Lesson 1
_____	Finding the Main Idea	
_____	Recalling Facts	
_____	Making Inferences	
_____	Using Words Precisely	
_____	**Reading Comprehension Score**	

Author's Approach

Put an X in the box next to the correct answer.

1. The authors use the first sentence of the article to

☒ a. introduce the setting of the article.

☐ b. describe the qualities of old whaling ships.

☐ c. compare whaling and fishing.

2. What do the authors mean by the statement "The crew of the *Essex* was used to working in dangerous conditions"?

☐ a. The crew was mistreated by their captain.

☒ b. The crew understood how whales had to be hunted.

☐ c. The crew disliked their jobs.

3. What is the authors' purpose in writing "A Whale of a Tale"?

☐ a. to encourage the reader to visit an aquarium that has whales

☒ b. to inform the reader about whaling methods

☐ c. to tell an exciting story about a whale

4. Which of the following statements from the article best describes conditions on Henderson's Island?

☐ a. By a stroke of pure luck, the three boats had drifted toward a tiny island.

☐ b. The island wasn't on any map.

☒ c. The island had fresh water, but almost no food.

_____ Number of correct answers

Record your personal assessment of your work on the Critical Thinking Chart on page 58.

Summarizing and Paraphrasing

Follow the directions provided for questions 1 and 2. Put an X in the box next to the correct answer for question 3.

1. Look for the important ideas and events in paragraphs 4 and 5. Summarize those paragraphs in one or two sentences.

_____

_____

_____

2. Complete the following one-sentence summary of the article using the lettered phrases from the phrase bank below. Write the letters on the lines.

Phrase Bank

a. how a whale attacked the *Essex*

b. what happened to the whalers after the attack

c. the whalers' attempts to kill a whale

The article "A Whale of a Tale" begins with ___A___, goes on to explain ___B___, and ends with ___C___.

3. Choose the sentence that correctly restates the following sentence from the article: "When the two other whaleboats returned from the hunt, the men were stunned to find the *Essex* lying on its side."

☒ a. The crews of the other two whaleboats were very surprised to find the *Essex* lying on its side when they came back from the hunt.

☐ b. The crew of the *Essex* was shocked when the two other whaleboats returned to the side of the injured ship.

☐ c. The hunt was over when the two other whaleboats returned to the *Essex*.

_____ Number of correct answers

Record your personal assessment of your work on the Critical Thinking Chart on page 58.

Critical Thinking

Follow the directions provided for questions 1, 3, and 4. Put an X in the box next to the correct answer for the other questions.

1. For each statement below, write *O* if it expresses an opinion or write *F* if it expresses a fact.

___O___ a. Someone should have killed the whale because it was too violent.

___O___ b. The men of the *Essex* were braver than most people would be in that situation.

___F___ c. Whales usually don't attack humans.

2. Judging by the descriptions in the article, you can conclude that the following happened after passing ships rescued the survivors:

☐ a. The crew decided never to tell anyone what happened.

☒ b. The crew told their rescuers the story of their adventure.

☐ c. The crew immediately forgot about their adventures.

3. Choose from the letters below to correctly complete the following statement. Write the letters on the lines.

In the article, _____ and _____ are alike.

a. the reason why the whaleboat needed repair

b. the reason why only three men stayed on the island

c. the reason why the *Essex* sank

4. Choose from the letters below to correctly complete the following statement. Write the letters on the lines.

According to the article, _____ caused the ship to _____, and the effect was _____.

a. the crew were set adrift in the middle of the ocean

b. sink

c. whale's attack on the *Essex*

5. What did you have to do to answer question 3?

☐ a. find an opinion (what someone thinks about something)

☐ b. find a description (how something looks)

☐ c. find a comparison (how things are the same)

_____ Number of correct answers

Record your personal assessment of your work on the Critical Thinking Chart on page 58.

Personal Response

If I were the authors, I would add _____

_____

because _____

_____

_____

Self-Assessment

While reading the article, I found it easiest to _____

_____

_____

_____

_____

CRITICAL THINKING

Grizzly Tales

Bill Riodan didn't see the bear until it was too late. Riodan had been out hunting deer in the Alaskan woods. On his way home, he came to a big spruce tree lying on the ground. He set his gun down and began to climb over the fallen tree. As he did so, a huge paw reached up from the other side of the log. Riodan felt panic rising in his chest. He was perched right over the den of a grizzly bear! With a quick swipe, the bear dug her claws into Riodan's back and pulled him down to the ground.

The adult grizzly bear can grow more than eight feet tall and weigh more than 1,500 pounds. While on a hike in the western states or Alaska, you'd better hope you don't run into one of these unpredictable animals.

2   There was nothing Riodan could do. The bear began to rip open his body. She took bite after bite from his arms, neck, and back. She ate chunks of flesh the size of fists. In effect, the bear was eating him alive!

3   Within a few minutes, Riodan passed out. When he awoke, the bear was still there. Now her two cubs were poking at him. Riodan tried to get up, but as soon as he moved, the mother bear pounced on him again. She grabbed him by the leg and shook him, crushing his leg bone between her jaws.

4   Again Riodan passed out. The next time he woke up, it was night. He didn't know if the bears had gone away or were just sleeping. Slowly, quietly, he crawled away. He dragged himself to a creek. Hours later, friends found him there, inching his way downstream.

5   Riodan's body was covered with 42 wounds. Muscles had been torn from his shoulders, arms, and neck. His leg was badly mangled. He was lucky to be alive. Doctors said it was the creek that saved him. The mud and leaves there helped seal the wounds and stop the bleeding.

6   Bill Riodan's brush with death came in the fall of 1908. Riodan was not the first person to be attacked by a bear. And he certainly wasn't the last. Every year or two, someone is killed in a bear attack. Often the killer is a grizzly. These animals, also called Alaskan brown bears, are found throughout the western United States. They are huge creatures. In fact, they are the largest meat-eating animal that lives on land. Standing over eight feet tall, they can weigh up to 1,500 pounds. Sometimes they run away when they see a human being. But sometimes they attack.

7   Deane and Lorraine Lengkeek found that out the hard way. They were walking through Montana's Glacier National Park on August 30, 1991. As they rounded a bend, they saw a mother grizzly and her two cubs. The Lengkeeks dropped to the ground. They had heard that the best way to avoid a bear attack was to play dead.

8   But this mama bear was not fooled. She gave a low growl. Then she raced over to Deane Lengkeek. She bit into his side with her enormous yellow teeth. Holding him in her mouth, she shook her head a couple of times. Then she threw him into the air. When he hit the ground, she picked him up again. She began to haul him back into the bushes.

9   "Oh, dear God, not like this!" he cried out. "Please, not like this!"

10   Lorraine Lengkeek was terrified. She did the only thing she could think of to do. She ran after the bear, swinging her binoculars over her head. When she got close, she hit the animal's nose with the binoculars. After four blows, the grizzly dropped Deane. Now the bear turned toward Lorraine. Lorraine swung the binoculars again. After this blow, the grizzly finally turned and ran off.

11   Deane Lengkeek was badly hurt, but he survived. He owed his life to his wife's brave actions. Perhaps Lorraine was successful because she targeted the nose. It is a very sensitive part of a bear's body. Bears don't have good eyesight. They can't hear well, either. So they rely heavily on their keen sense of smell. They need their long noses to help them sniff out danger and food. Sometimes when a bear's nose is hurt, the bear retreats. A few people have fought off bears by

jamming their fingers into bears' nostrils.

12 Sometimes, though, bears have been almost impossible to stop. In 1905, three Alaskans began shooting at a grizzly that attacked them. Thirteen times they struck the bear with bullets. Again and again the bear fell down. But each time it got back up. Finally, after the 14th shot, the bear dropped to the ground for good.

13 Claude Barnes had his rifle in his hands when a grizzly came at him. Barnes was out hunting in the Wyoming woods. He had just taken a shot at a small bear. The mother bear heard its yelp. She came charging toward Barnes. Said Barnes, "I shot at her heart while she . . . stood towering over me." That didn't stop her, though. She dropped onto all fours and kept coming. "I reloaded as quickly as I could and fired into her face. She was right on me . . . she grabbed the gun barrel with her teeth [and] knocked me down with her body. . . . Her great jaws [sank] into my side just below my right shoulder. . . . A huge foot was placed on my shoulders and I could smell the hot breath of the tremendous brute."

14 Barnes had fired two bullets at the bear at very close range. Yet neither one seemed to slow the animal down. Barnes survived only because the bear suddenly turned to check on her wounded cub. Knowing that grizzlies don't climb trees, Barnes scrambled up a nearby pine. The bear tried to reach him, but she couldn't. So she stood on the ground, clawing angrily at the trunk. Barnes clung to that tree for hours. At last, his bullets took effect. The bear collapsed, dead, a few feet from the tree.

15 Game warden Al Johnson also knew that grizzlies don't climb trees. In 1973 Johnson wanted to take some pictures of bear cubs. He climbed 15 feet into a tree, sure that he would be safe there. But he was wrong. A mother grizzly with three cubs came along. When the mother detected Johnson's presence, she became enraged. She flew at the tree with fury. She managed to get high enough to pull Johnson to the ground. She bit his shoulder, arms, and elbow. Then she tore a patch of skin off his scalp. He heard her teeth scraping against his skull. At last, the bear turned away. Rather than finish Johnson off, she chose to lead her cubs away to safety.

16 Could any of these attacks have been prevented? Perhaps. Bears usually don't pounce unless they feel threatened. Claude Barnes provoked his attacker by shooting at her cub. Bill Riodan upset his bear by coming too close to her nest. The problem is that it doesn't take much to threaten a bear.

Just going into the woods can do it. That's all Deane and Lorraine Lengkeek did. And it's all Al Johnson did. So the next time you're out enjoying a nature walk, keep your fingers crossed that you don't cross paths with a grizzly.

If you have been timed while reading this article, enter your reading time below. Then turn to the Words-per-Minute Table on page 55 and look up your reading speed (words per minute). Enter your reading speed on the graph on page 56.

Reading Time: Lesson 2

—————— : ——————
Minutes   *Seconds*

A | Finding the Main Idea

One statement below expresses the main idea of the article. One statement is too general, or too broad. The other statement explains only part of the article; it is too narrow. Label the statements using the following key:

M—Main Idea   **B—Too Broad**   **N—Too Narrow**

<u>M</u>   1. People who go hiking in the woods should always be prepared to handle dangerous situations there.

<u>B</u>   2. Because of their great size and defensive nature, grizzly bears are always a threat to people in the woods.

<u>N</u>   3. One man survived a bear attack because his wife drove off the bear by striking its nose.

_____ Score 15 points for a correct M answer.

_____ Score 5 points for each correct B or N answer.

_____ **Total Score:** Finding the Main Idea

B | Recalling Facts

How well do you remember the facts in the article? Put an X in the box next to the answer that correctly completes each statement about the article.

1. In 1908 Bill Riodan survived a bear attack by
   - ☐ a. shooting at the bear and scaring it away.
   - ☐ b. outrunning the bear.
   - ☒ c. dragging himself into a creek.

2. Alaskan brown bears are found
   - ☐ a. only in Alaska.
   - ☒ b. throughout the western United States.
   - ☐ c. throughout North America.

3. When Deane and Lorraine Lengkeek came upon a mother bear and her cubs, they tried to fool her by
   - ☒ a. playing dead.
   - ☐ b. waving their hands over their heads to make themselves look taller.
   - ☐ c. making a great deal of noise.

4. It is *not* true that grizzly bears
   - ☐ a. have a keen sense of smell.
   - ☐ b. have poor eyesight.
   - ☒ c. can climb trees.

5. When game warden Al Johnson climbed a tree,
   - ☐ a. an attacking bear climbed up after him.
   - ☒ b. a bear reached high and pulled him down.
   - ☐ c. a bear knocked the tree down.

Score 5 points for each correct answer.

_____ **Total Score:** Recalling Facts

C **Making Inferences**

When you combine your own experience with information from a text to draw a conclusion that is not directly stated in that text, you are making an inference. Below are five statements that may or may not be inferences based on information in the article. Label the statements using the following key:

C—Correct Inference   **F—Faulty Inference**

C 1. Mother grizzly bears feel that human beings who come near are a danger to their cubs.

F 2. No one should ever go walking in the woods.

F 3. Usually, grizzly bears attack people because they are hungry and see people as a tasty treat.

P 4. Hikers can feel safe on trails through wooded areas if they carry handguns for protection against bears.

F 5. Grizzly bears have a short attention span.

Score 5 points for each correct answer.

_____ **Total Score:** Making Inferences

 D **Using Words Precisely**

Each numbered sentence below contains an underlined word or phrase from the article. Following the sentence are three definitions. One definition is closest to the meaning of the underlined word. One definition is opposite or nearly opposite. Label those two definitions using the following key; do not label the remaining definition.

C—Closest   **O—Opposite or Nearly Opposite**

1. Riodan tried to get up, but as soon as he moved, the mother bear <u>pounced</u> on him again.

    O a. set free

    C b. swiftly seized

    _____ c. rolled

2. Perhaps Lorraine was successful because she <u>targeted</u> the nose.

    _____ a. admired

    O b. overlooked; ignored

    C c. aimed at

3. So they <u>rely</u> heavily on their keen sense of smell.

    C a. depend on

    _____ b. wait for

    O c. distrust

4. Sometimes when a bear's nose is hurt, the bear <u>retreats</u>.

    _____ a. growls

    O b. advances

    C c. falls back

5. Claude Barnes <u>provoked</u> his attacker by shooting at her cub.

_____C_____ a. angered

_____O_____ b. soothed

_____ c. discussed

_____ Score 3 points for each correct C answer.

_____ Score 2 points for each correct O answer.

_____ **Total Score:** Using Words Precisely

Enter the four total scores in the spaces below, and add them together to find your Reading Comprehension Score. Then record your score on the graph on page 57.

Score	Question Type	Lesson 2
_____	Finding the Main Idea	
_____	Recalling Facts	
_____	Making Inferences	
_____	Using Words Precisely	
_____	**Reading Comprehension Score**	

Author's Approach

Put an X in the box next to the correct answer.

1. The main purpose of the first paragraph is to

☐ a. explain why the bear attacked the hunter.

☐ b. show how careless the hunter had been.

☒ c. describe the suddenness of the bear attack.

2. Which of the following statements from the article best describes Alaskan brown bears?

☒ a. In fact, they are the largest meat-eating animal that lives on land.

☐ b. Knowing that grizzlies don't climb trees, Barnes scrambled up a nearby pine.

☐ c. Often the killer is a grizzly.

3. Judging by statements from the article "Grizzly Tales," you can conclude that the authors want the reader to think that

☐ a. grizzlies never attack unless the victim has purposely annoyed them.

☐ b. grizzlies are naturally cruel animals.

☒ c. grizzly attacks cannot be predicted.

4. The authors tell this story mainly by

☐ a. comparing different topics.

☒ b. telling different stories about the same topic.

☐ c. using their imagination and creativity.

_____ Number of correct answers

Record your personal assessment of your work on the Critical Thinking Chart on page 58.

Summarizing and Paraphrasing

Follow the directions provided for questions 1 and 2. Put an X in the box next to the correct answer for question 3.

1. Look for the important ideas and events in paragraphs 7 and 8. Summarize those paragraphs in one or two sentences.

_____

_____

_____

2. Reread paragraph 11 in the article. Below, write a summary of the paragraph in no more than 25 words.

_____

_____

_____

_____

3. Choose the sentence that correctly restates the following sentence from the article: "Barnes had fired two bullets at the bear at very close range."

☐ a. The two bullets that Barnes had fired hit a very close range.

☐ b. Barnes closed his hand on his rifle and fired two bullets.

☐ c. Barnes was very close to the bear when he fired two bullets at it.

_____ Number of correct answers

Record your personal assessment of your work on the Critical Thinking Chart on page 58.

Critical Thinking

Put an X in the box next to the correct answer for questions 1, 3, and 4. Follow the directions provided for the other questions.

1. From what the article told about Deane and Lorraine Lengkeek's encounter with the angry grizzly, you can predict that the couple will

☐ a. go on camping trips in the Alaskan woods every year.

☒ b. probably avoid long walks in grizzly country from now on.

☐ c. become active in organizations that protect the grizzly bear.

2. Choose from the letters below to correctly complete the following statement. Write the letters on the lines.

In the article, _____ and _____ tried to escape the bear by taking the same action.

a. Claude Barnes

b. Al Johnson

c. Deane Lengkeek

3. What was the cause of the mother bear's attack on Claude Barnes?

☐ a. Barnes was walking in the woods near the bear.

☐ b. Barnes had shot at her cub.

☐ c. Barnes had climbed a tree.

CRITICAL THINKING

4. Which of the following theme categories would this article fit into?

☐ a. We must respect the strength and power of wild animals..

☐ b. Wild animals fear and hate humans.

☐ c. Modern humans have no appreciation for nature.

5. Which paragraphs from the article provide evidence that supports your answer to question 2?

_____

_____ Number of correct answers

Record your personal assessment of your work on the Critical Thinking Chart on page 58.

Personal Response

Begin the first 5–8 sentences of your own article about a frightening walk in the woods. It may tell of a real experience or one that is imagined.

_____

_____

_____

_____

Self-Assessment

I'm proud of my answer to question _____ in the _____ section because _____

_____

_____

_____

Attack of the Red Fire Ants

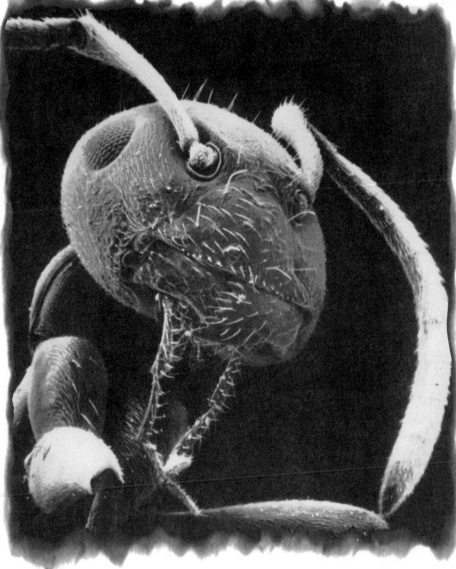

In Alabama a newborn baby was killed while lying in a crib. In Florida a little girl lost her life as she played with her dog. In Louisiana an old man died after being attacked in a motel room. What did these victims have in common? They were all killed by red fire ants.

2 At first glance these ants don't look very dangerous. They are small—only about an eighth of an inch long. They have big heads and skinny legs. But the size and shape of the ants is not

The red fire ant is so small that you can't see it well without a powerful electron microscope. However, these ants have been causing big problems in the Southeast and are now traveling to other states too.

the problem. The little critters have a couple of secret weapons. First of all, each ant has two claws near its mouth. It can use these claws to grab onto your skin. Also, it has a stinger at the back end of its body. This stinger carries poison. As the ant clings to your skin, it can shoot the poison right into you.

3   The sting of a single red fire ant does not hurt that much. According to one researcher, "It [is] worse than a mosquito bite but nowhere near as bad as a wasp sting." But the sting is only the beginning. As the poison enters your body, your skin will start to itch. The itching will build to a burning feeling. Finally, a yellow blister will break out at the spot where you were stung. This nasty blister can linger for days, even weeks. It will itch like crazy. But beware: scratching will only make it worse. The blister could become infected. You could end up scarred for the rest of your life.

4   One fire ant sting is bad enough. But you almost never get stung once. When a red fire ant attacks, it stings again and again. And these ants don't travel alone. So when one latches onto you, you can be pretty sure that dozens of others will join in. In just a few seconds, you can be covered with a whole swarm of stinging ants.

5   Marion Bernhardt found that out the hard way. She was lying in a Florida hospital in 1994. Suddenly, from out of nowhere, red fire ants began to crawl all over her. Said Bernhardt, "I was stung all up and down my legs, and I had welts all over them and on my side. They burned for days. I never had such an experience in all my life." Many people can sympathize with Bernhardt. Each year, more than 60,000 victims seek medical help after being stung by red fire ants. Millions of others suffer quietly at home.

6   Marion Bernhardt didn't die from her stings. Most people don't. They can get stung hundreds of times and still walk away. But others react more strongly to the poison. For them, red fire ants can spell death. These people may have trouble breathing after they've been stung. They may pass out or go into shock. Before you know it, they're dead. Red fire ant stings have caused the deaths of more than 85 people in the United States since the 1930s.

7   Human beings are not the only targets of red fire ants. The ants will go after beetles, rats, birds, even small cows. Their goal is to kill and then eat their victims. One of their favorite meals is the flesh of young deer. Fire ants find these deer quite easy to kill. When a fawn is threatened, it stands perfectly still. That allows the fire ants to climb onto it. They sting it everywhere—on its legs, its stomach, its neck. As the ants sting the fawn near its eyes, it becomes blinded. Finally, it reacts by trying to lick the ants off its body. But that just makes matters worse. The ants keep ejecting their poison even as they are swallowed. They sting the inside of the deer's mouth. They sting its throat, windpipe, and stomach. Soon these body parts swell up so that the fawn can no longer breathe. Within minutes, it is dead.

8   Americans didn't always have to worry about red fire ants. Before 1930 there were none in the United States. They made their homes in the forests of Brazil. But one day the ants got

onto a ship bound for Alabama. When the ship docked, the ants came pouring out onto the land.

9   At first, they stayed in the Southeast. They could be found only in Alabama, Mississippi, and Florida. Lately, though, they've turned up in other places. They've slipped into moving vans and trucks. Some have made it all the way to California. They've also crept north to Tennessee and Virginia.

10   Red fire ants used to stay outdoors. But as Marion Bernhardt can tell you, they are now coming inside. They get into hospitals and motels. They crawl under the floor mats of cars. They cause accidents by stinging drivers. They chew through electrical wires in houses. Some people have even fled their homes to get away from the dreaded ants.

11   As if all this were not enough, there's another problem on the horizon. Something creepy is going on with America's red fire ants. In the past, these ants formed regular ant colonies. Each colony had a single queen. She was the only one who could lay eggs. The rest of the ants in the group would fight to protect her. They would kill any other queen who came near. Because of this, each colony built its mound far away from any other colony.

12   Now that is changing. No one knows why, but some colonies are beginning to accept more than one queen. As many as 500 queens have been found in a single mound. These colonies are huge. One queen can lay 100 eggs an hour. So how many eggs can 500 queens lay? The total is more than a million a day! As these eggs hatch, ants spill out of the mound and start colonies of their own.

13   Multiqueen colonies don't mind having neighbors. Again, no one knows why. But ants in these groups don't fight with nearby colonies. So new fire ant mounds are springing up right next to old ones. In some places, you can find up to 500 colonies in a single acre. Each colony inhabits a mound that is about a foot high. Each contains millions of ants. You can just imagine what your backyard would look like if several colonies of fire ants set up house there.

14   Where will it end? Will red fire ants keep spreading across America? Will their colonies keep getting bigger and closer together? It's hard to say. But one thing's for sure. If red fire ants come to your neighborhood, you'll know it!

A | Finding the Main Idea

One statement below expresses the main idea of the article. One statement is too general, or too broad. The other statement explains only part of the article; it is too narrow. Label the statements using the following key:

M—Main Idea   **B—Too Broad**   **N—Too Narrow**

_____ 1. Even though they are not a major public safety problem, red fire ants should be considered dangerous.

_____ 2. A growing problem in the United States, red fire ants, originally from Brazil, can sting and even kill their victims.

_____ 3. When they first came to the United States, red fire ants stayed mostly in the southeastern states.

_____ Score 15 points for a correct M answer.

_____ Score 5 points for each correct B or N answer.

_____ **Total Score:** Finding the Main Idea

B | Recalling Facts

How well do you remember the facts in the article? Put an X in the box next to the answer that correctly completes each statement about the article.

1. Each red fire ant has two claws near its
   ☐ a. front legs.
   ☒ b. mouth.
   ☐ c. antennae.

2. The blister caused by red fire ants sting can last for
   ☒ a. days or weeks.
   ☐ b. years.
   ☐ c. the rest of your life.

3. Since coming to the United States, red fire ants have caused the deaths of about
   ☒ a. 85 people.
   ☐ b. 60,000 people.
   ☐ c. one million people.

4. Red fire ants can kill a fawn easily because it
   ☐ a. doesn't notice the stings.
   ☐ b. falls asleep after it is stung once.
   ☒ c. stands still and lets the ants climb over it.

5. One change taking place among red fire ants is that
   ☐ a. huge wars are breaking out among colonies.
   ☒ b. colonies are accepting more than one queen.
   ☐ c. the ants are changing in color and size.

Score 5 points for each correct answer.

_____ **Total Score:** Recalling Facts

C Making Inferences

When you combine your own experience with information from a text to draw a conclusion that is not directly stated in that text, you are making an inference. Below are five statements that may or may not be inferences based on information in the article. Label the statements using the following key:

C—Correct Inference   **F—Faulty Inference**

_____ 1. If red fire ants hadn't gotten on that ship bound for Alabama, they probably never would have come to the United States.

_____ 2. When red fire ants attack a fawn, the final cause of death is a lack of oxygen.

_____ 3. Little animals are always more dangerous than they seem to be at first glance.

_____ 4. Red fire ants clearly show an ability to change and adapt to their surroundings.

_____ 5. If you don't irritate red fire ants, they will leave you alone.

Score 5 points for each correct answer.

_____ **Total Score:** Making Inferences

D Using Words Precisely

Each numbered sentence below contains an underlined word or phrase from the article. Following the sentence are three definitions. One definition is closest to the meaning of the underlined word. One definition is opposite or nearly opposite. Label those two definitions using the following key; do not label the remaining definition.

C—Closest   **O—Opposite or Nearly Opposite**

1. Many people can <u>sympathize with</u> Bernhardt.

_____ a. live near

_____ b. share or understand the feelings of

_____ c. disagree with

2. The ants keep <u>ejecting</u> their poison even as they are swallowed.

_____ a. holding inside

_____ b. making

_____ c. shooting out

3. But one day the ants got onto a ship <u>bound for</u> Alabama.

_____ a. headed toward

_____ b. going away from

_____ c. built in

4. Some people have even fled their homes to get away from the <u>dreaded</u> ants.

_____ a. feared

_____ b. busy

_____ c. welcomed

5. Each colony <u>inhabits</u> a mound that is about a foot high.

_____ a. creates

_____ b. lives in

_____ c. moves away from

_____ Score 3 points for each correct C answer.

_____ Score 2 points for each correct O answer.

_____ **Total Score:** Using Words Precisely

Enter the four total scores in the spaces below, and add them together to find your Reading Comprehension Score. Then record your score on the graph on page 57.

Score	Question Type	Lesson 3
_____	Finding the Main Idea	
_____	Recalling Facts	
_____	Making Inferences	
_____	Using Words Precisely	
_____	**Reading Comprehension Score**	

Author's Approach

Put an X in the box next to the correct answer.

1. The main purpose of the first paragraph is to

☐ a. express an opinion about red fire ants.

☐ b. describe red fire ants.

☒ c. show how widespread the problem of red fire ants has become.

2. What do the authors mean by the statement "Many people can sympathize with Bernhardt"?

☒ a. Like Bernhardt, many people have been stung by red fire ants.

☐ b. Many people like Bernhardt.

☐ c. Many people have met Bernhardt.

3. Which of the following statements from the article best describes the diet of red fire ants?

☐ a. When a red fire ant attacks, it stings again and again.

☒ b. The ants will go after beetles, rats, birds, even small cows.

☐ c. They are small—only about an eighth of an inch long.

4. The authors probably wrote this article to

☒ a. inform readers about a growing problem with red fire ants.

☐ b. persuade readers not to live in any southern state.

☐ c. entertain readers with a humorous story.

_____ Number of correct answers

Record your personal assessment of your work on the Critical Thinking Chart on page 58.

Summarizing and Paraphrasing

Follow the directions provided for questions 1 and 2. Put an X in the box next to the correct answer for question 3.

1. Look for the important ideas and events in paragraphs 9 and 10. Summarize those paragraphs in one or two sentences.

_____

_____

_____

2. Complete the following one-sentence summary of the article using the lettered phrases from the phrase bank below. Write the letters on the lines.

Phrase Bank

a. one red fire ant attack and the history of the spread of red fire ants

b. a description of red fire ants and their stings

c. an explanation of the changes that are taking place in red fire ant colonies

---

The article "Attack of the Red Fire Ants" begins with __A__, goes on to describe __B__, and ends with __C__.

3. Choose the best one-sentence paraphrase for the following sentence from the article: "Human beings are not the only targets of red fire ants."

☐ a. Humans are the only creatures who need to fear red fire ants.

☐ b. Red fire ants target only human beings.

☒ c. Red fire ants attack both humans and many other creatures.

_____ Number of correct answers

Record your personal assessment of your work on the Critical Thinking Chart on page 58.

Critical Thinking

Put an X in the box next to the correct answer for questions 1, 2, 4, and 5. Follow the directions provided for question 3.

1. Which of the following statements from the article is an opinion rather than a fact?

☐ a. As many as 500 queens have been found in a single mound.

☒ b. [The red fire ant's sting] is worse than a mosquito bite but nowhere near as bad as a wasp sting.

☐ c. When a fawn is threatened, it stands perfectly still.

2. From the article, you can predict that if fawns would run away from red fire ants,

☐ a. the ants would kill them even more quickly.

☒ b. they would have a better chance of surviving an attack.

☐ c. there would soon be more fawns than red fire ants.

3. Choose from the letters below to correctly complete the following statement. Write the letters on the lines.

   According to the article, _____ and _____ are alike in that there are red fire ants in both states.

   a. Virginia

   b. Mississippi

   c. Pennsylvania

4. What was the effect of red fire ants boarding a ship in Brazil?

   ☒ a. The ants were brought to Alabama.

   ☐ b. The ants began to enjoy traveling in ocean-going ships.

   ☐ c. The ants began to attack sailors.

5. What did you have to do to answer question 2?

   ☐ a. find an opinion (what someone thinks about something)

   ☐ b. find a description (how something looks)

   ☒ c. make a prediction (what might happen next)

_____ Number of correct answers

Record your personal assessment of your work on the Critical Thinking Chart on page 58.

Personal Response

Describe a time when you were stung, attacked, or really bothered by insects.

_____

_____

_____

_____

Self-Assessment

From reading this article, I have learned _____

_____

_____

_____

Snakes, Snakes Everywhere

You never know where you'll find one. You might see one in your garden in New Jersey. You could spot one in a river in South America.

You might even find one in your toilet in India. Some of the snakes you run across may be harmless. But many are dangerous.A few are downright deadly. It is estimated that snakes kill 15,000 people each year.

2   Some snakes can kill you by wrapping themselves around your body. They squeeze so hard that they cut off your air supply. That's what pythons do. These snakes are

This trusting mouse may soon learn a fatal lesson about the eating habits of its companion, the boa constrictor.

enormous. They can be up to 32 feet long. And they can weigh well over 300 pounds. You can find pythons in lots of places. They live in Australia, Africa, and Asia.

3   Like other snakes, pythons are deaf. They have good eyesight, but they'd have no trouble finding you even in the dark. That's because they could sense your body heat as you walked by. Pythons use their lips to pick up and locate the source of any body heat. Then they zero in on it. They lunge forward with their jaws stretched wide. A python could easily sink its sharp, backward-pointing teeth into your skin. Then it would wind its body around you. Tighter and tighter it would wrap itself, squeezing its muscles as hard as it could. The result would be a death grip that would force all the air out of your body. It wouldn't take long for you to suffocate to death.

4   Pythons don't often go after human beings. Normally they feed on smaller animals. But every now and then, one breaks the mold. In 1979, for instance, a python waited in a grassy plain in South Africa. A teenage boy walked past, herding some cattle. All at once,

the python struck. It moved like lightning. It drove its teeth through the boy's flesh. Then it coiled itself around his body. In minutes, the boy was dead.

5   Boa constrictors kill the same way as the python does. Other snakes, though, use a different method. They kill you by injecting poison into your body. This poison, called venom, is what a cobra would use to kill you.

6   Cobras live in Asia and Africa. Like pythons, they are very big. Sometimes they grow to be about 18 feet long. The sight of a cobra in its attack pose is something you'll never forget. It lifts its head up from its coiled body. It stares at you with eyes that do not blink. The skin near its head puffs out, creating its famous "hood." When a cobra bites, venom flows from two fangs in its mouth. This venom quickly attacks your nerves. It can stop your heart. It can also paralyze your lungs.

7   Some cobras deliver their venom without biting. Three kinds of African cobras spit venom. They do this only when they feel threatened. But if you ever bother one—even accidentally—

watch out! These cobras can hit targets from up to nine feet away. They aim for the eyes. And they don't very often miss. If you get this venom in your eyes, you'll quickly go blind. Your sight may return after a while . . . or you may be blinded for life.

8   Rattlesnakes have deadly venom too. Their venom can stop your heart and lungs. It can also cause bleeding inside your body. It can turn your kidneys and other organs to mush.

9   A rattlesnake will try to warn you if you come too close. It will shake the "rattle" on its tail. If you don't take the hint and move away, the rattlesnake may strike. Like the cobra, it has needle-sharp fangs. These teeth can cut right through leather shoes. One "rattler" proved that in 1988. A 12-year-old boy stepped on the snake near his Florida home. The snake's fangs pierced the boy's shoe and dug into his foot right near the anklebone. The boy almost died from the effects of the venom.

10   Rattlesnakes can make their move in the blink of an eye. In fact, the rattlesnake has the fastest attack time of any poisonous snake. In less than one second it can spring forward, bite, and draw back again. It moves so quickly that you may not see it. You will feel it, though. A rattlesnake's bite feels like hot needles being jabbed into your skin.

11   It takes about one teaspoon of rattlesnake venom to kill an adult human being. But it takes only a drop or two from a snake called the taipan. This snake lives in Australia. It may grow to 10 feet in length. It has orange eyes and a head shaped like a coffin. Taipans feed on mice, rats, and other small creatures. But they'll go after anything that disturbs them.

12   In 1991 Clive Brady was walking near Australia's Barron River. He came face to face with a taipan. Brady scrambled to get out of its way. But he wasn't fast enough. The snake reared up and bit his leg. Its jaws worked like a jackhammer, giving Brady seven quick bites. Then it let go and disappeared into the bushes.

13   Brady tried to walk toward help. But he didn't get far. Luckily, another man was down by the river that day. He rushed to get help for Brady. Nevertheless, by the time Brady arrived at the nearby hospital, he was in great pain. He couldn't stand. He was seeing double. His body was covered with sweat. His stomach was clenched tight. And his lungs were seizing up.

14   Doctors gave Brady medicine to fight the taipan's poison. But the venom had already caused bleeding inside his body. For hours Brady bled from the fang marks on his leg. He also bled heavily from his gums. It took six

hours for doctors to stop the bleeding. At last, they announced that Brady would live. He was very lucky. It could easily have gone the other way.

15   The medicine that saved Clive Brady is called antivenom. Doctors have come up with antivenom for all types of snakebites. But if you don't get it in time, it won't do you any good. The best thing to do, of course, is to avoid being bitten in the first place. But there are 300 kinds of poisonous snakes in the world. Add them to the snakes that can suffocate you, and you end up with a long list under the heading Do Not Disturb.

A | Finding the Main Idea

One statement below expresses the main idea of the article. One statement is too general, or too broad. The other statement explains only part of the article; it is too narrow. Label the statements using the following key:

M—Main Idea   **B—Too Broad**   **N—Too Narrow**

_B_ 1. The "hood" of the cobra is formed when the snake puffs out the skin near its head, which happens when the snake is in its attack pose.

_M_ 2. Snakes are among the creatures most dangerous to human beings.

_B_ 3. Pythons, rattlesnakes, cobras, and other types of snakes attack people, killing their victims either by squeezing them to death or poisoning them.

_____ Score 15 points for a correct M answer.

_____ Score 5 points for each correct B or N answer.

_____ **Total Score:** Finding the Main Idea

B | Recalling Facts

How well do you remember the facts in the article? Put an X in the box next to the answer that correctly completes each statement about the article.

1. A python can kill you by
☐ a. wrapping itself around you and squeezing.
☐ b. injecting poison into you with its fangs.
☐ c. biting until you bleed to death.

2. A python senses the body heat of a victim
☐ a. through its skin.
☐ b. with its nose.
☐ c. with its lips.

3. Another snake that kills as a python does is the
☐ a. rattlesnake.
☐ b. boa constrictor.
☐ c. cobra.

4. When a rattlesnake strikes, it
☐ a. moves with blinding speed.
☐ b. always goes for your eyes.
☐ c. follows up the strike by rattling its tail.

5. You may survive a snakebite if you
☐ a. seat the skin around the bite.
☐ b. heat the skin around the bite.
☐ c. receive the right antivenom quickly.

Score 5 points for each correct answer.

_____ **Total Score:** Recalling Facts

C | Making Inferences

When you combine your own experience with information from a text to draw a conclusion that is not directly stated in that text, you are making an inference. Below are five statements that may or may not be inferences based on information in the article. Label the statements using the following key:

C—Correct Inference   F—Faulty Inference

_____ 1. You could scare pythons away by making a great deal of noise.

_____ 2. You could protect yourself against most dangerous snakes by wearing thick leather all around your body.

_____ 3. A good way to study a rattlesnake's attack is to film it and then show the film in slow motion.

_____ 4. The bigger a person is, the better chance he or she has of surviving an attack by a snake.

_____ 5. If you survive a rattlesnake bite, you are immune to the venom of other snakes.

Score 5 points for each correct answer.

_____ **Total Score:** Making Inferences

D | Using Words Precisely

Each numbered sentence below contains an underlined word or phrase from the article. Following the sentence are three definitions. One definition is closest to the meaning of the underlined word. One definition is opposite or nearly opposite. Label those two definitions using the following key; do not label the remaining definition.

C—Closest   O—Opposite or Nearly Opposite

1. Pythons use their lips to pick up and locate the source of any body heat.

_____ a. outcome
_____ b. beginning
_____ c. nature

2. Then it coiled itself around his body.

_____ a. pounded
_____ b. wound in a spiral; curled
_____ c. straightened

3. Rattlesnakes have deadly venom too.

_____ a. likely to cause death
_____ b. likely to cure or make better
_____ c. powerful

4. It wouldn't take long for you to suffocate to death.

_____ a. bleed
_____ b. breathe deeply
_____ c. smother

5. The snake's fangs <u>pierced</u> the boy's shoe and dug into his foot right near the anklebone.

_____ a. withdrew

_____ b. dislodged

_____ c. ran through

_____ Score 3 points for each correct C answer.

_____ Score 2 points for each correct O answer.

_____ **Total Score:** Using Words Precisely

Enter the four total scores in the spaces below, and add them together to find your Reading Comprehension Score. Then record your score on the graph on page 57.

Score	Question Type	Lesson 4
_____	Finding the Main Idea	
_____	Recalling Facts	
_____	Making Inferences	
_____	Using Words Precisely	
_____	**Reading Comprehension Score**	

Author's Approach

Put an X in the box next to the correct answer.

1. What is the authors' purpose in writing "Snakes, Snakes Everywhere"?

☐ a. to convey a frightening mood

☐ b. to inform the reader about dangerous snakes

☐ c. to emphasize the similarities between rattlesnakes and boa constrictors

2. Which of the following statements from the article best describes the taipan?

☐ a. It has orange eyes and a head shaped like a coffin.

☐ b. The skin near its head puffs out, creating its famous 'hood.'

☐ c. It will shake the "rattle" on its tail.

3. From the statements below, choose the one that you believe the authors would agree with.

☐ a. All snakes are dangerous.

☐ b. All snakes attack and kill humans using the same methods.

☐ c. After you have been bitten by a snake, it is important to get medical help quickly.

_____ Number of correct answers

Record your personal assessment of your work on the Critical Thinking Chart on page 58.

Summarizing and Paraphrasing

Put an X in the box next to the correct answer for question 1. Follow the directions provided for question 2.

1. Below are summaries of the article. Choose the summary that says all the most important things about the article but in the fewest words.

☐ a. Some kinds of snakes can kill people by squeezing them, and others kill their victims by poisoning them with venom. If you are bitten by a snake, seek medical help as quickly as possible.

☐ b. Pythons and boa constrictors kill their victims by squeezing them until they suffocate. Rattlesnakes try to warn people not to get too close by rattling their tails. The rattlesnake can spring forward, bite, and draw back in less than a second.

☐ c. Snakes can be dangerous in many ways. Try not to disturb any snakes you may find.

2. Reread paragraph 7 in the article. Below, write a summary of the paragraph in no more than 25 words.

_____

_____

_____

_____

Reread your summary and decide whether it covers the important ideas in the paragraph. Next, try to shorten the summary to 15 words or less without leaving out any essential information. Write this summary below.

_____

_____

_____

_____ Number of correct answers

Record your personal assessment of your work on the Critical Thinking Chart on page 58.

Critical Thinking

Follow the directions provided for questions 1, 3, and 5. Put an X in the box next to the correct answer for the other questions.

1. For each statement below, write O if it expresses an opinion or write F if it expresses a fact.

_____ a. Snakes are sneaky hunters.

_____ b. Antivenom is medicine that can save the lives of snakebite victims.

_____ c. It takes only a drop or two of taipan venom to kill an adult human.

2. From the information in paragraph 13, you can predict that

☐ a. Brady will be angry with the man who took him to the hospital, because he interfered.

☐ b. Brady will quickly forget his encounter with the taipan.

☐ c. Brady will remember his brush with death and thank the man who took him to the hospital.

3. Using what you know about pythons and what is told about cobras in the article, name three ways a python is similar to and three ways a python is different from a cobra. Cite the paragraph number(s) where you found details in the article to support your conclusions.

Similarities

_____

_____

_____

Differences

_____

_____

_____

4. What was one effect of the taipan's bite on Clive Brady?

☐ a. He began to see double.

☐ b. He forgot his name.

☐ c. His heart stopped.

5. In which paragraph did you find your information or details to answer question 4? _____

_____ Number of correct answers

Record your personal assessment of your work on the Critical Thinking Chart on page 58.

Personal Response

How do you think you would feel if you heard a rattling sound as you were walking in the desert? What would you do?

_____

_____

_____

_____

Self-Assessment

I was confused on question _____ in the _____ section because

_____

_____

_____

_____

Rhinos vs. Humans

Not long ago, a tailor in Nepal needed some cloth. He set off for the market to buy it. The road took him through the Chitwan National Park. It was a path the tailor had walked many times before. He knew he had to be careful. Often he had seen or heard a rhinoceros in this area. The tailor knew that a startled rhino is a dangerous thing. If one decided to charge, it could easily trample him. In the past, the tailor had scared rhinos off by screaming. If that failed, he climbed a tree and waited until the animal went away.

The largest of all rhinoceroses is the white rhinoceros. This beast can weigh more than three tons. By comparison, a small car weighs about one ton. Like a car, a rhino does a lot of damage when it hits something at high speed.

2   On this morning, however, the tailor's luck ran out. He heard a rhino coming his way. It was a female with a young calf. The mother rhino must have sensed a threat, because all of a sudden she charged. The tailor leaped out of the way, grabbing an overhead tree branch. He tucked his legs up and wrapped them around the branch. He hung there, six feet off the ground, as the rhino rushed by. The animal's head was just high enough to hit him. She knocked him out of the tree. Turning around, the rhino trampled the tailor with her hooves. Then, using her sharp teeth, she ripped open the man's belly.

3   We know about the tailor because he didn't die right away. His cries caught the ear of a man named Purney, who rushed to the tailor's aid. The tailor showed Purney his wound and told him what had happened. He asked Purney for a drink of water. Using his hat, Purney brought some water from a nearby stream. He then ran for help. But by the time he got back with some rescuers, the tailor was dead.

4   Purney told this tale to a nature writer named Fiona Sunquist. She retold it in her 1987 book Tiger Moon. Sunquist also wrote about her own close call. It was with a male rhino that had already killed two people. This beast was so famous that people had given him his own name—Triscar.

5   One day Sunquist hid in a tiny grove of trees. She wanted to photograph a young rhino as it wallowed in a mud hole. Soon three adult rhinos also showed up. One was Triscar. Sunquist turned her camera on him. Although he did not see her, he headed toward the trees where she was hiding. "I stared in horror as his bulk filled, then overflowed, the viewfinder," she wrote. "He was six feet away, then two, and finally his nose touched the branches. All I could hear was the sound of his breath."

6   Triscar began eating some leaves inches from where Sunquist crouched. She thought she was going to die. Although rhinos have poor eyesight, they have a keen sense of smell. Sunquist figured the rhino would pick up her scent and kill her. But he didn't. The wind must have been blowing the other way. He never noticed her. After a while, he just

moved away. Sunquist was left shaking with fear in a pool of sweat.

7   As the case of the tailor showed, Sunquist had reason to be afraid. Rhinos can and do attack human beings. This is especially true of a strong male or a female with her calf. These animals can be provoked by a slight sound or smell. It really does not take much. Sometimes they seem to charge for no reason at all. Unfortunately, people can get caught in the way. More human beings are killed by rhinos each year than by tigers or leopards.

8   If given the choice, rhinos would probably stay away from people altogether. After all, rhinos are not meat eaters. They have nothing to gain by attacking people. But the opposite is not true. People kill rhinos all the time. They go out of their way to do it. It's not because they need the meat. It's not because they fear for their lives. It's because they're trying to make money.

9   Poachers want rhino horns. Buyers will pay thousands of dollars for one. A horn can earn an African poacher enough money to live for a year. Some buyers turn the horns into knife handles for rich customers. Others use the horns to make expensive medicines.

10   With all the poaching, rhinos are fighting for their lives. Once they

roamed Asia and Africa in great numbers. Today they are just barely hanging on. In Asia there are three kinds of rhinos. Put together, they add up to fewer than 2,000. Things are not much better in Africa. There are two kinds of African rhinos, the black and the white. Their numbers add up to fewer than 11,000.

11   To save the rhinos, officials have moved most of them to special parks. But that has not stopped all poachers. The money is so good that some are willing to take their chances. They sneak into the parks to kill the rhinos. Some African governments have struck back. In 1985 Zimbabwe launched Operation Stronghold. It was a drastic step. Park rangers could shoot poachers on sight. "Make no mistake," said one park warden. "We are fighting a very nasty bush war here, with no quarter given."

12   The ranger wasn't blowing smoke. He was dead serious. One morning two poachers shot a rhino in the Zambezi River Valley. The blast of their guns pierced the morning silence. Alerted, two park rangers moved in. They found the bloody trail of a dying black rhino. They also spotted two sets of footprints. These belonged to the poachers who had shot the rhino.

13   The rangers followed the trail. They snuck up on the poachers. As the poachers bent to cut off the rhino's

horn, the rangers closed to within 15 yards. Again, gunshots rang out. One of the poachers fell dead. The other tried to hide, but the rangers shot him, too.

14   At the end of two years, rangers had killed 13 poachers. "[The poachers] are the enemy," said one park official. "And we destroyed them."

15   Whose life is more precious— a human being's or a rhino's? It is sad that the question is even raised. But it doesn't have to be that way. Poachers wouldn't shoot rhinos if no one bought rhino-horn knives or medicines. Many nations have joined the fight to stop the trade of rhino products. Still, some people break the law. Rhino horns continue to be sold on the black market. That spells bad news for the few rhinos left in the wild.

If you have been timed while reading this article, enter your reading time below. Then turn to the Words-per-Minute Table on page 55 and look up your reading speed (words per minute). Enter your reading speed on the graph on page 56.

Reading Time: Lesson 5

——————— : ———————
Minutes   Seconds

A Finding the Main Idea

One statement below expresses the main idea of the article. One statement is too general, or too broad. The other statement explains only part of the article; it is too narrow. Label the statements using the following key:

M—Main Idea   **B—Too Broad**   **N—Too Narrow**

_____ 1. Rhinos do not attack people for food, but if they are upset, they will charge and kill people.

_____ 2. Rhinos and human beings do not get along well when members of the two groups are close together.

_____ 3. There are fewer than 15,000 rhinos alive in the whole world.

_____ Score 15 points for a correct M answer.

_____ Score 5 points for each correct B or N answer.

_____ **Total Score:** Finding the Main Idea

B Recalling Facts

How well do you remember the facts in the article? Put an X in the box next to the answer that correctly completes each statement about the article.

1. A tailor in Nepal was killed by a
   ☐ a. man-hunting rhino.
   ☐ b. mother rhino.
   ☐ c. mother rhino and her baby.

2. Fiona Sunquist had a close call with a rhino when she
   ☐ a. was writing a book.
   ☐ b. talked with the man who had helped the tailor.
   ☐ c. tried to photograph it.

3. Sunquist survived the encounter because
   ☐ a. the wind was blowing the right way.
   ☐ b. rhinos have a poor sense of smell.
   ☐ c. the rhino was unusually mild.

4. More people are killed by rhinos each year than by
   ☐ a. cancer.
   ☐ b. tigers or leopards.
   ☐ c. traffic accidents.

5. Officials have moved most rhinos to special parks in order to
   ☐ a. protect people from the rhinos.
   ☐ b. protect the rhinos from people.
   ☐ c. make it easier for scientists to study rhinos.

Score 5 points for each correct answer.

_____ **Total Score:** Recalling Facts

C Making Inferences

When you combine your own experience with information from a text to draw a conclusion that is not directly stated in that text, you are making an inference. Below are five statements that may or may not be inferences based on information in the article. Label the statements using the following key:

C—Correct Inference   F—Faulty Inference

_____ 1. One way to escape an angry rhino is to climb a strong, tall tree.

_____ 2. It's impossible to tell the difference between one full-grown rhino and another.

_____ 3. If officials can stop poachers from attacking rhinos, the number of rhinos in Africa and Asia will probably increase.

_____ 4. When people know there are wild rhinos in an area, they recognize the possible dangers and stay away.

_____ 5. In the end, the people responsible for poaching are the people who buy rhino-horn products.

Score 5 points for each correct answer.

_____ **Total Score:** Making Inferences

D Using Words Precisely

Each numbered sentence below contains an underlined word or phrase from the article. Following the sentence are three definitions. One definition is closest to the meaning of the underlined word. One definition is opposite or nearly opposite. Label those two definitions using the following key; do not label the remaining definition.

C—Closest   O—Opposite or Nearly Opposite

1. The tailor knew that a <u>startled</u> rhino is a dangerous thing.

_____ a. surprised

_____ b. hungry

_____ c. bored

2. <u>Poachers</u> want rhino horns.

_____ a. people who bring back animals

_____ b. nature writers

_____ c. people who steal or kill animals

3. Once they <u>roamed</u> Asia and Africa in great numbers.

_____ a. wandered freely throughout

_____ b. were limited to one place in

_____ c. attacked

4. "I stared in horror as his bulk filled, then <u>overflowed</u>, the viewfinder," she wrote.

_____ a. moved to the far side of

_____ b. shrank within; drained from

_____ c. increased past the limits of

5. In 1985 Zimbabwe launched Operation Stronghold. It was a <u>drastic</u> step.

_____ a. limited

_____ b. extreme

_____ c. difficult

_____ Score 3 points for each correct C answer.

_____ Score 2 points for each correct O answer.

_____ **Total Score:** Using Words Precisely

Enter the four total scores in the spaces below, and add them together to find your Reading Comprehension Score. Then record your score on the graph on page 57.

Score	Question Type	Lesson 5
_____	Finding the Main Idea	
_____	Recalling Facts	
_____	Making Inferences	
_____	Using Words Precisely	
_____	**Reading Comprehension Score**	

Author's Approach

Put an X in the box next to the correct answer.

1. The authors probably wrote this article to

☐ a. celebrate the fact that rhinos are dying out.

☐ b. call attention to the rhino's problems with survival.

☐ c. entertain readers with an exciting story.

2. Choose the statement below that is the weakest argument for killing rhinos.

☐ a. Rhinos often attack and kill human beings.

☐ b. Rhino horns can be used to make medicines.

☐ c. Rhino horns can be made into handsome knife handles.

3. What do the authors imply by saying "With all the poaching, rhinos are fighting for their lives"?

☐ a. Rhinos are beginning to poach in order to survive.

☐ b. Rhinos are organizing attacks on poachers in order to survive.

☐ c. The number of rhinos in the world today has fallen because poachers are killing these animals.

4. Choose the statement below that best describes the authors' position in paragraph 15.

☐ a. A human being's life is more precious than a rhino's life.

☐ b. If people continue to buy and sell rhino products, the rhino may not survive.

☐ c. Soon all nations will ban the trade of rhino products.

_____ Number of correct answers

Record your personal assessment of your work on the Critical Thinking Chart on page 58.

CRITICAL THINKING

Summarizing and Paraphrasing

Follow the directions provided for question 1. Put an X in the box next to the correct answer for questions 2 and 3.

1. Complete the following one-sentence summary of the article using the lettered phrases from the phrase bank below. Write the letters on the lines.

> **Phrase Bank**
> a. a description of efforts to stop poaching
> b. reasons why rhinos are have trouble surviving
> c. a story of a rhino attack

The article "Rhinos vs. Humans" begins with _____, goes on to explain _____, and ends with _____.

2. Below are summaries of the article. Choose the summary that says all the most important things about the article but in the fewest words.

☐ a. Rhinos can be dangerous to humans, sometimes attacking and killing them. However, people are even more dangerous to rhinos, killing them for their horns. Some nations are punishing poachers, but trade in rhino products continues.

☐ b. Even though rhinos are dangerous to humans, as in the case of a tailor who was attacked by a rhino in the Chitwan National Park not long ago, they should be protected. In 1985 in Zimbabwe, some poachers were shot and killed.

☐ c. Rhinos kill more human beings every year than tigers or leopards do. Rhino horns can be used in expensive medicines.

3. Choose the sentence that correctly restates the following sentences from the article: "The ranger wasn't blowing smoke. He was dead serious."

☐ a. The ranger never smoked in the park because he firmly believed that smoking was dangerous.

☐ b. The ranger wasn't fooling.

☐ c. The ranger died when he inhaled too much smoke.

> _____ Number of correct answers
>
> Record your personal assessment of your work on the Critical Thinking Chart on page 58.

Critical Thinking

Put an X in the box next to the correct answer for questions 1, 2, 4, and 5. Follow the directions provided for question 3.

1. Which of the following statements from the article is an opinion rather than a fact?

☐ a. More human beings are killed by rhinos each year than by tigers or leopards.

☐ b. A horn can earn an African poacher enough money to live for a year.

☐ c. Whose life is more precious—a human being's or a rhino's? It is sad that the question is even raised.

2. Judging by the events in the article, you can predict that the following will happen next:

☐ a. Poachers will continue to break the law and kill rhinos.

☐ b. Poachers will soon realize that rhinos are in danger and will stop killing them.

☐ c. Nations will change their laws to allow hunters to kill as many rhinos as they want to.

3. Reread paragraph 2. Then choose from the letters below to correctly complete the following statement. Write the letters on the lines.

According to paragraph 2, _____ because _____.

a. the rhino believed that her calf was in danger

b. the rhino attacked the tailor

c. the tailor shot at the rhino's calf

4. How is this article about rhinos related to the theme of *Angry Animals*?

☐ a. It explains that rhinos are dying out rapidly.

☐ b. It tells that rhinos sometimes attack and kill humans when they feel threatened.

☐ c. It says that rhinos are protected from poachers in many countries.

5. What did you have to do to answer question 3?

☐ a. find an opinion (what someone thinks about something)

☐ b. find a description (how something looks)

☐ c. find a cause (why something happened)

_____ Number of correct answers

Record your personal assessment of your work on the Critical Thinking Chart on page 58.

Personal Response

This article is different from other articles about angry animals I've read because _____

_____

and Fiona Sunquist is unlike other people in those articles who came face to face with wild animals because _____

_____

Self-Assessment

I can't really understand how _____

_____

_____

_____

Compare and Contrast

Think about the articles you have read in Unit One. Pick the three animal attacks that you believe were most surprising or unexpected. Write the titles of the articles that tell about them in the first column of the chart below. Use information you learned from the articles to fill in the empty boxes in the chart.

Title	When and where did the animal attack?	What caused the animal to attack?	What did the animal do to its victim when it attacked?

One person in the article _____ could have been prepared for a possible attack. If I were in that situation, I would

protect myself by _____

_____

_____

Words-per-Minute Table

Unit One

Directions: If you were timed while reading an article, refer to the Reading Time you recorded in the box at the end of the article. Use this Words-per-Minute Table to determine your reading speed for that article. Then plot your reading speed on the graph on page 56.

Lesson No. of Words	Sample 648	1 1,226	2 1,185	3 1,101	4 1,069	5 1,082	
1:30	432	817	790	734	713	721	**90**
1:40	389	736	711	661	641	649	**100**
1:50	353	669	646	601	583	590	**110**
2:00	324	613	593	551	535	541	**120**
2:10	299	566	547	508	493	499	**130**
2:20	278	525	508	472	458	464	**140**
2:30	259	490	474	440	428	433	**150**
2:40	243	460	444	413	401	406	**160**
2:50	229	433	418	389	377	382	**170**
3:00	216	409	395	367	356	361	**180**
3:10	205	387	374	348	338	342	**190**
3:20	194	368	356	330	321	325	**200**
3:30	185	350	339	315	305	309	**210**
3:40	177	334	323	300	292	295	**220**
3:50	169	320	309	287	279	282	**230**
4:00	162	307	296	275	267	271	**240**
4:10	156	294	284	264	257	260	**250**
4:20	150	283	273	254	247	250	**260**
4:30	144	272	263	245	238	240	**270**
4:40	139	263	254	236	229	232	**280**
4:50	134	254	245	228	221	224	**290**
5:00	130	245	237	220	214	216	**300**
5:10	125	237	229	213	207	209	**310**
5:20	122	230	222	206	200	203	**320**
5:30	118	223	215	734	194	197	**330**
5:40	114	216	209	194	189	191	**340**
5:50	111	210	203	189	183	185	**350**
6:00	108	204	198	184	178	180	**360**
6:10	105	199	192	179	173	175	**370**
6:20	102	194	187	661	169	171	**380**
6:30	100	189	182	169	164	166	**390**
6:40	97	184	178	165	160	162	**400**
6:50	95	179	173	161	156	158	**410**
7:00	93	175	169	157	153	155	**420**
7:10	90	171	165	154	149	151	**430**
7:20	88	167	162	150	146	148	**440**
7:30	86	163	158	147	143	144	**450**
7:40	85	160	155	144	139	141	**460**
7:50	83	157	151	141	136	138	**470**
8:00	81	153	148	138	134	135	**480**

Minutes and Seconds

Seconds

Plotting Your Progress: Reading Speed

Unit One

Directions: If you were timed while reading an article, write your words-per-minute rate for that article in the box under the number of the lesson. Then plot your reading speed on the graph by putting a small X on the line directly above the number of the lesson, across from the number of words per minute you read. As you mark your speed for each lesson, graph your progress by drawing a line to connect the X's.

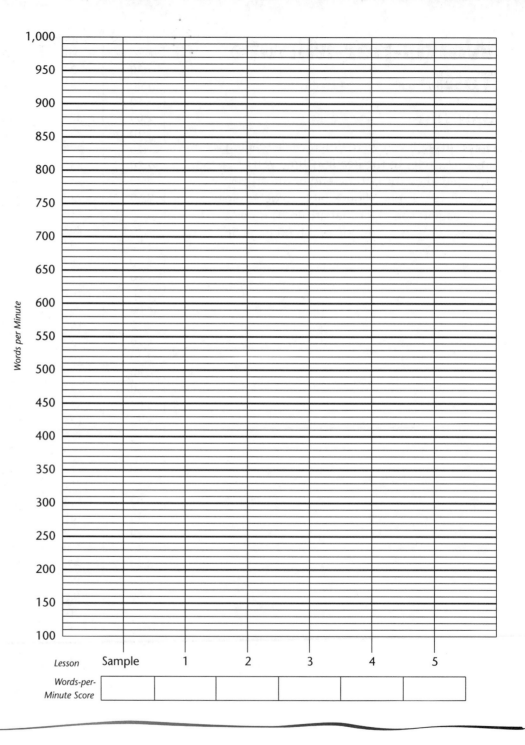

Plotting Your Progress: Reading Comprehension

Unit One

Directions: Write your Reading Comprehension score for each lesson in the box under the number of the lesson. Then plot your score on the graph by putting a small X on the line directly above the number of the lesson and across from the score you earned. As you mark your score for each lesson, graph your progress by drawing a line to connect the X's.

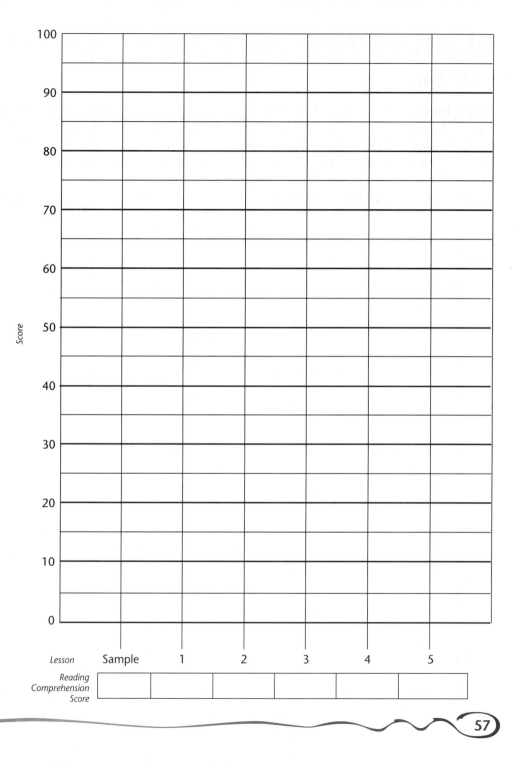

Plotting Your Progress: Critical Thinking

Unit One

Directions: Work with your teacher to evaluate your responses to the Critical Thinking questions for each lesson. Then fill in the appropriate spaces in the chart below. For each lesson and each type of Critical Thinking question, do the following: Mark a minus sign (–) in the box to indicate areas in which you feel you could improve. Mark a plus sign (+) to indicate areas in which you feel you did well. Mark a minus-slash-plus sign (–/+) to indicate areas in which you had mixed success. Then write any comments you have about your performance, including ideas for improvement.

Lesson	Author's Approach	Summarizing and Paraphrasing	Critical Thinking
Sample			
1			
2			
3			
4			
5			

UNIT TWO

Danger–Rabid Animals!

Kelly Ahrendt did not feel well. She told her mother that her knuckles hurt and her left arm and shoulder ached. So on July 8, 1993, Margaret Ahrendt took her 11-year-old daughter to see a doctor. The doctor found a slight ear infection and a possible strep throat. But it was nothing serious. The doctor also thought Kelly might have pulled a muscle. She was an athletic girl. She often did cartwheels outdoors on the family farm in New York. "It was no big deal," said Margaret. "[The doctor] said it was OK to go on vacation."

When an animal such as this raccoon has rabies, it can spread the disease to nearby human beings. Untreated rabies will quickly kill human victims if treatment isn't started right away.

2   Everyone thought that Kelly would soon be her old self again. The next day the family set out on a camping trip in upstate New York, near Lake George. But Kelly didn't improve. In fact, she began to get sicker. She grew feverish. Her pains intensified. Then Kelly began having strange visions. "First she was crying, and then the crying stopped and she just started talking crazy," said her mother. "[Kelly screamed], 'The flies, get the flies off me!' And then she said she saw worms on her."

3   Margaret and her husband Richard were desperate. They took Kelly to three hospital emergency rooms. But doctors could do nothing to stop her severe pain. Her muscles twitched violently. And her horrible visions grew worse. She was disgusted at the thought of her own hair. She even drew back whenever her parents came near. "I'm sorry," she told them. "I know I shouldn't be afraid of you, but I can't help it."

4   On July 11, Kelly Ahrendt died.

5   What caused this young girl's death? At first, the doctors had no idea. It was only later that the hard truth became clear. Laboratory tests showed that Kelly had died from rabies. She was the first person in New York to die from the disease since 1954.

6   Rabies is a deadly disease. Caused by a virus, it can strike most mammals—including humans. An animal with rabies passes it on to others by biting or scratching. Pets such as dogs and cats can have rabies. In fact, dogs are the greatest rabies threat in much of the world. Still, it is rare for dogs in the United States to have rabies. Here, most dogs and cats are vaccinated against the disease. So the real threat comes from wild animals. Raccoons, foxes, skunks, and other creatures can all catch the disease.

7   An animal with rabies—called a rabid animal—is not always easy to identify. It may look tame or just a bit sick. It might have trouble walking. You might see it do something odd. For instance, a night animal like a raccoon might be walking down the street in the middle of the day. If you ever run across such a creature, beware! It might be suffering from the most common strain of rabies, called the dumb strain. Victims of this strain often act slow-witted. Although your first impulse may be to help such an animal, *don't do it*. You can't save a rabid animal, and you'll only put yourself at risk.

8   The other form of rabies is much easier to recognize. It is the *furious* strain. A dog with this type of rabies will foam at the mouth. It will howl constantly. It may wander for long distances. And it will attack for no reason at all. Any dog with furious rabies is as angry as an animal can get. That's where the expression *mad dog* comes from.

9   Rabies in humans is difficult to diagnose. That's because the virus doesn't travel through the blood stream. If it did, it would show up in a blood test. Instead, rabies spreads through the nerve cells. The virus slowly works its way up to the brain. While this is happening, the victim shows no signs of the disease. This period can last anywhere from 10 days to seven months. The time frame depends on where the virus entered the body.

10 When rabies finally reaches the brain, symptoms appear. These include crazy fears, foaming at the mouth, and muscle spasms. By this time, it's too late for treatment. The disease at this point is always fatal. So even if the doctors had figured out what was wrong with Kelly Ahrendt, they couldn't have saved her. Once symptoms appear, death follows quickly. Most victims, like Kelly, die within a week.

11 The Ahrendts had known all about the threat of rabies. They knew that rabid raccoons had recently appeared in New York. Margaret had even read an article about a rabid cat to her seven children. She warned the children not to touch raccoons or other wild animals. "Kelly knew—all the kids knew—about the animals," Margaret said. "If they saw a raccoon, they'd usually all come screaming into the house."

12 So how did Kelly get the disease? At first, it was a total mystery. The Ahrendts had some animals on their farm. They had two cats, a dog, two horses, three rabbits, and some ducks and chickens. But none of these animals were rabid. If one had been, it would have died before Kelly did. And, given her mother's firm warning, it was not likely that Kelly got close enough to be bitten by a rabid raccoon.

13 In late August doctors finally solved the mystery. More lab tests showed that Kelly had gotten rabies from a bat. It turned out that bats lived in the attic of the family home. But no one knew exactly how Kelly had come into contact with the bats. Did one of them bite or scratch her? Maybe not. A bite or a scratch isn't always necessary. It is possible for bats with rabies to send the virus through the air. Two people are known to have picked up rabies this way. They got it just by breathing the air in caves filled with rabid bats.

14 People infected with rabies don't have to die. But steps must be taken *before* the symptoms start. So if you ever suspect you've been exposed to rabies, see a doctor—quickly! There is a cure. It was developed by Louis Pasteur in 1885. For a long time, this cure involved a grim treatment. Victims had to have a series of 14 to 21 injections in the stomach. Today the cure is more bearable. It consists of five shots in the arm. That treatment still may sound pretty painful. But when you think of the alternative, it's not hard to roll up your sleeve and face the needle.

If you have been timed while reading this article, enter your reading time below. Then turn to the Words-per-Minute Table on page 101 and look up your reading speed (words per minute). Enter your reading speed on the graph on page 102.

Reading Time: Lesson 6

_____ : _____
Minutes   Seconds

A | Finding the Main Idea

One statement below expresses the main idea of the article. One statement is too general, or too broad. The other statement explains only part of the article; it is too narrow. Label the statements using the following key:

M—Main Idea   **B—Too Broad**   **N—Too Narrow**

_____ 1. In 1993 Kelly Ahrendt became the first person in New York to die from rabies since 1954.

_____ 2. There are some diseases that can be passed from animals to human beings, including rabies.

_____ 3. Rabies, a disease that attacks the nervous system, almost always kills the people who catch it from animal carriers.

_____ Score 15 points for a correct M answer.

_____ Score 5 points for each correct B or N answer.

_____ **Total Score:** Finding the Main Idea

B | Recalling Facts

How well do you remember the facts in the article? Put an X in the box next to the answer that correctly completes each statement about the article.

1. Signs of Kelly Ahrendt's sickness included
   - ☐ a. fever, aching joints, and coughing.
   - ☐ b. pulled muscles and earache.
   - ☐ c. fever, pain, and crazy visions.

2. An animal with rabies can pass it on by biting
   - ☐ a. or scratching.
   - ☐ b. alone.
   - ☐ c. or licking.

3. In the United States, pet dogs and cats rarely pass rabies on to human beings because they
   - ☐ a. are rarely in wild areas.
   - ☐ b. get along well with their owners.
   - ☐ c. are vaccinated against rabies.

4. In the so-called dumb strain of rabies, a dog will
   - ☐ a. foam at the mouth.
   - ☐ b. act sick and walk slowly.
   - ☐ c. never bark.

5. A person who shows symptoms of rabies
   - ☐ a. is likely to pass it along to others.
   - ☐ b. must be given oxygen.
   - ☐ c. is already past treatment.

Score 5 points for each correct answer.

_____ **Total Score:** Recalling Facts

C Making Inferences

When you combine your own experience with information from a text to draw a conclusion that is not directly stated in that text, you are making an inference. Below are five statements that may or may not be inferences based on information in the article. Label the statements using the following key:

C—Correct Inference   F—Faulty Inference

_____ 1. The first doctor that the Ahrendts went to is responsible for Kelly's death.

_____ 2. Kelly's visions were a sign that the rabies had entered the brain.

_____ 3. Some other countries do not require pets to be vaccinated against rabies.

_____ 4. A dog that howls constantly probably has rabies.

_____ 5. Different viruses attack different systems within the human body.

Score 5 points for each correct answer.

_____ **Total Score:** Making Inferences

D Using Words Precisely

Each numbered sentence below contains an underlined word or phrase from the article. Following the sentence are three definitions. One definition is closest to the meaning of the underlined word. One definition is opposite or nearly opposite. Label those two definitions using the following key; do not label the remaining definition.

C—Closest   O—Opposite or Nearly Opposite

1. She grew feverish. Her pains intensified.

_____ a. came and went in flashes
_____ b. lessened
_____ c. became stronger

2. When rabies finally reaches the brain, symptoms appear.

_____ a. lack of clues
_____ b. signs
_____ c. imaginary friends

3. But think of the alternative.

_____ a. other choice
_____ b. unexpected event
_____ c. necessity; only possibility

4. But no one knew exactly how Kelly had come into contact with the bats.

_____ a. separation from
_____ b. a feeling of dislike toward
_____ c. touch with

5. So if you ever suspect you've been <u>exposed to</u> rabies, see a doctor—quickly!

_____ a. made allergic to

_____ b. brought close to

_____ c. removed far from

_____

_____	Score 3 points for each correct C answer.
_____	Score 2 points for each correct O answer.
_____	**Total Score:** Using Words Precisely

Enter the four total scores in the spaces below, and add them together to find your Reading Comprehension Score. Then record your score on the graph on page 103.

Score	Question Type	Lesson 6
_____	Finding the Main Idea	
_____	Recalling Facts	
_____	Making Inferences	
_____	Using Words Precisely	
_____	**Reading Comprehension Score**	

Author's Approach

Put an X in the box next to the correct answer.

1. The main purpose of the first paragraph is to

☐ a. show how harmless rabies seems in its early stages.

☐ b. explain how Kelly Ahrendt got rabies.

☐ c. find fault with Kelly Ahrendt's doctor for not spotting her rabies right away.

2. Which of the following statements from the article best describes dogs with dumb rabies?

☐ a. Victims of this strain often act slow-witted.

☐ b. [The dog] will howl constantly.

☐ c. A dog with this type of rabies will foam at the mouth.

3. From the statements below, choose those that you believe the authors would agree with.

☐ a. Rabies is not a very serious disease.

☐ b. People who get rabies always die of the disease.

☐ c. Rabies is curable if it is treated quickly.

4. In this article, "Everyone thought that Kelly would soon be her old self again" means

☐ a. Kelly's family wanted her to stop acting foolishly.

☐ b. Kelly's family expected her to recover from her illness.

☐ c. everyone expected Kelly to start acting more grown up.

_____ Number of correct answers

Record your personal assessment of your work on the Critical Thinking Chart on page 104.

Summarizing and Paraphrasing

Follow the directions provided for question 1. Put an X in the box next to the correct answer for the other questions.

1. Look for the important ideas and events in paragraphs 12 and 13. Summarize those paragraphs in one or two sentences.

_____

_____

_____

_____

2. Read the statement from the article below. Then read the paraphrase of that statement. Choose the reason that best tells why the paraphrase does not say the same thing as the statement.

   Statement: Lab tests showed that Kelly Ahrendt got rabies from a bat.

   Paraphrase: Doctors think that Kelly Ahrendt got rabies by breathing in the rabies virus sent out by the bats in her attic.

   ☐ a. Paraphrase says too much.

   ☐ b. Paraphrase doesn't say enough.

   ☐ c. Paraphrase doesn't agree with the statement.

3. Choose the sentence that correctly restates the following sentence from the article: "Rabies in humans is difficult to diagnose."

   ☐ a. It is difficult to diagnose any disease, but especially rabies, in humans.

   ☐ b. No one can tell whether humans have rabies or not.

   ☐ c. It's hard to know whether a person has rabies or not.

_____ Number of correct answers

Record your personal assessment of your work on the Critical Thinking Chart on page 104.

Critical Thinking

Put an X in the box next to the correct answer for questions 1 and 4. Follow the directions provided for the other questions.

1. Which of the following statements from the article is an opinion rather than a fact?

   ☐ a. When rabies finally reaches the brain, symptoms appear.

   ☐ b. But when you think of the alternative, it's not hard to roll up your sleeve and face the needle.

   ☐ c. An animal with rabies passes it on to others by biting or scratching.

2. Choose from the letters below to correctly complete the following statement. Write the letters on the lines.

In the article _____ and _____ are different.

   a. the fate of rabies victims who get the 14-shot rabies cure

   b. the fate of rabies victims who get the five-shot rabies cure

   c. the fate of rabies victims who don't get any treatment

3. Think about cause-effect relationships in the article. Fill in the blanks in the cause-effect chart, using the letters below.

Cause	Effect
_____	Rabies doesn't show up in blood tests.
Rabies can make a dog seem angry.	_____
Once symptoms appear, rabies can't be cured.	_____

   a. Dogs with rabies are sometimes called mad dogs.

   b. Rabies does not travel in the blood stream.

   c. Dogs who show symptoms will die soon.

4. What did you have to do to answer question 2?

☐ a. find an opinion (what someone thinks about something)

☐ b. find a description (how something looks)

☐ c. find a contrast (how things are different)

_____ Number of correct answers

Record your personal assessment of your work on the Critical Thinking Chart on page 104.

Personal Response

Would you recommend this article to other students? Explain.

_____

_____

_____

_____

Self-Assessment

Which concepts or ideas from the article were difficult to understand?

_____

_____

_____

Which were easy?

_____

_____

_____

_____

Night Killers

They come out at night. Flying just three feet over the ground, they are constantly on the lookout for blood. Their four white fangs glisten in the light of the moon. They hunt by sound and by smell. As they swoop past, they make an angry sputtering noise. These night killers are vampire bats. You don't want to be around when they're out looking for a meal.

2   Vampire bats live in Central America and parts of Mexico. They are not very big. Most weigh only about one ounce. Their bodies are just three

Like the mythical creature it was named for, the vampire bat drinks its victims' blood. This bat usually ignores humans, preferring to drink the blood of large animals. But in a pinch, it looks for blood wherever it can find it.

inches long, or the size of a human thumb. Even with their wings stretched out, they are only eight inches wide. Still, these tiny creatures can kill a cow. Just ask Cesar Murillo, a cattle rancher in Mexico. In 1995 vampire bats killed more than 50 cows in his herd. Using heat sensors in the nose, vampire bats find a vein close to the surface of the victim's skin. Legend says they suck the blood out of their victim. But that isn't true. Instead, they use their sharp teeth to cut the flesh. Often they make their incision behind an ear, an elbow, or a hoof. Then they lick the blood from the open wound. Vampire bats can drink their own body weight in warm blood at one meal. That can take a while. Sometimes their gory feast will last as long as 20 minutes.

3   Because vampire bats come out at night, their victims are usually asleep at the time of the attack. The bats have a special chemical in their saliva. It numbs the victim's skin. That way, they can sink their teeth in without waking the victim. The bats use a second chemical to keep the blood from drying up while they eat.

4   The real trouble with these nasty creatures isn't the blood they take away. It's the diseases they leave behind. Vampire bats carry several deadly diseases, including rabies. That's how they killed Cesar Murillo's cows. As they lapped up the cows' blood, they infected the cows with rabies.

5   Within a few days, the cows began to act very strange. Murillo described how the disease affects cows. "They start to lose their ability to walk," he said. "Their back legs buckle when they try to stand. Then they start trying to crawl. They get this desperate look in their eyes. A short time later, they die."

6   As bad as the situation was for Murillo, it was much worse for people in Nicaragua. There, in 1999, vampire bats started to attack humans. One morning, the parents of two young girls woke up to find vampire bats drinking the blood of their sleeping daughters. In another case, a small girl died from rabies after being attacked by vampire bats. In all, the bats attacked at least 22 people.

7   These attacks were most unusual. Vampire bats prefer the blood of large birds, cows, horses, and pigs. They live in deep caves or old wells. So normally they don't go near humans. But in 1998 Hurricane Mitch struck Nicaragua. That storm brought record-breaking rains. Many caves and wells were flooded. Bats were forced out of their rural homes and into places where people lived. (Heavy rains had also helped trigger the outbreak of bat attacks on cows in Mexico.)

8   In one Nicaraguan town, people had to fight the bats for several months. "Every night they're after us," said one farmer. "The cows, the horses, and us too."

9   Many people in the town rubbed garlic on their animals. Aris Mejia explained why. Mejia was one of a dozen bat killers hired by the government. "The bats just don't like the odor [of garlic]," he said. "[But] it only lasts one night. If you don't put fresh garlic on the animals the next night, the bats come back."

10   Mejia found a more permanent solution. His job was to kill as many vampire bats as he could. He started hunting each night as soon as the sun

went down. Slaying bats wasn't a nice job. "It's kind of strange work, and not everyone in Nicaragua likes to do it," said Mejia. "You can always tell us by our scars." One vampire bat left an ugly scar on his left hand. It bit right through the thick gloves he was wearing.

11   Mejia didn't hunt vampire bats with a gun. He didn't try to expose them to the sunlight. And he didn't try to drive a stake through their hearts. Those weapons are used only in fiction when the villain is a human vampire. Instead, Mejia went after the bats with a net. If he could find where they lived, he would cover the entrance with his net. He could then trap the bats when they tried to come out.

12   If he couldn't find the bats' homes, Mejia used a different approach. He would have a farmer put all his animals in one corral. In this way, the cows, horses, and pigs would serve as bait. Then Mejia would wait. He knew the vampire bats would find them in a few nights. When they did, he would be waiting for them with his net.

13   After catching a bat, Mejia would smear it with poison and then let it go. The poison was strong enough to kill the bat, but it acted slowly. That was the plan. The released bat would fly back to its home. Other bats in the colony would then lick the poisoned bat in an attempt to clean it. Or sometimes the bats would fight and bite the poisoned bat. Either way, the others would swallow the poison. Within a few days all the bats in that colony would be dead. "For every bat we capture," said Mejia, "we can kill up to 10 or 15."

14   To many people, poisoning vampire bats sounds cruel. After all, most of the time these tiny creatures are not a big threat. They stay away from humans and attack only a few farm animals. But if heavy rains force the bats to look for food in other places, they become a huge problem. No one wants to wake up to find a vampire bat licking blood from his or her toes. When bats start to attack humans, bat killers such as Aris Mejia are in big demand.

If you have been timed while reading this article, enter your reading time below. Then turn to the Words-per-Minute Table on page 101 and look up your reading speed (words per minute). Enter your reading speed on the graph on page 102.

Reading Time: Lesson 7

———— : ————
Minutes   Seconds

A | Finding the Main Idea

One statement below expresses the main idea of the article. One statement is too general, or too broad. The other statement explains only part of the article; it is too narrow. Label the statements using the following key:

M—Main Idea   **B—Too Broad**   **N—Too Narrow**

_____ 1. Vampire bats drink animal blood. When floods bring them near farms and towns, they can cause the death of farm animals and humans by spreading disease.

_____ 2. Vampire bats are not usually dangerous, but they can become deadly in certain situations.

_____ 3. Vampire bats attacked 22 people in Nicaragua in 1999, causing the death of at least one girl.

_____ Score 15 points for a correct M answer.

_____ Score 5 points for each correct B or N answer.

_____ **Total Score:** Finding the Main Idea

B | Recalling Facts

How well do you remember the facts in the article? Put an X in the box next to the answer that correctly completes each statement about the article.

1. Vampire bats are about
   ☐ a. eight inches from head to toe.
   ☐ b. three inches from head to toe.
   ☐ c. three inches from the tip of one wing to the tip of the other wing.

2. Victims don't wake up when vampire bats lick their blood because the
   ☐ a. bats have a numbing chemical in their saliva.
   ☐ b. victims are already dead when the bats attack them.
   ☐ c. bats never break through the victims' skin.

3. The worst problem vampire bats cause is
   ☐ a. a loss of blood.
   ☐ b. the spread of diseases such as rabies.
   ☐ c. the poisoning of farm animals.

4. Bats don't like the smell of
   ☐ a. farm animals.
   ☐ b. human blood.
   ☑ c. garlic.

5. To kill bats, Aris Mejia
   ☐ a. smears them with poison.
   ☐ b. drives a stake through their hearts.
   ☐ c. shoots them with a gun.

_____ Score 5 points for each correct answer.

_____ **Total Score:** Recalling Facts

C | Making Inferences

When you combine your own experience with information from a text to draw a conclusion that is not directly stated in that text, you are making an inference. Below are five statements that may or may not be inferences based on information in the article. Label the statements using the following key:

C—Correct Inference   **F—Faulty Inference**

_____ 1. Vampire bats live alone and rarely contact other vampire bats.

_____ 2. Anyone who travels to Central America should expect a vampire bat attack.

_____ 3. In 1999 some people in Nicaragua slept with their windows open and with no screens on their windows.

_____ 4. If you are attacked by a vampire bat, you will probably get rabies.

_____ 5. Vampire bats sometimes bite humans when they are captured and frightened.

Score 5 points for each correct answer.

_____ **Total Score:** Making Inferences

D | Using Words Precisely

Each numbered sentence below contains an underlined word or phrase from the article. Following the sentence are three definitions. One definition is closest to the meaning of the underlined word. One definition is opposite or nearly opposite. Label those two definitions using the following key; do not label the remaining definition.

C—Closest   **O—Opposite or Nearly Opposite**

1. Sometimes their <u>gory</u> feast will last as long as 20 minutes.

_____ a. unusual and surprising

_____ b. clean and pleasant

_____ c. bloody and horrible

2. Heavy rains had also helped <u>trigger</u> the outbreak of bat attacks on cows in Mexico.

_____ a. set off

_____ b. stop

_____ c. discover

3. Mejia found a more <u>permanent</u> solution.

_____ a. shocking

_____ b. lasting

_____ c. temporary

4. <u>Slaying</u> bats wasn't a nice job.

_____ a. raising

_____ b. killing

_____ c. selling

5. When bats start to attack humans, bat killers such as Aris Mejia are <u>in big demand</u>.

_____ a. not needed

_____ b. trained

_____ c. wanted badly

_____ Score 3 points for each correct C answer.

_____ Score 2 points for each correct O answer.

_____ **Total Score:** Using Words Precisely

Enter the four total scores in the spaces below, and add them together to find your Reading Comprehension Score. Then record your score on the graph on page 103.

Score	Question Type	Lesson 7
_____	Finding the Main Idea	
_____	Recalling Facts	
_____	Making Inferences	
_____	Using Words Precisely	
_____	**Reading Comprehension Score**	

Author's Approach

Put an X in the box next to the correct answer.

1. What is the authors' purpose in writing "Night Killers"?

☐ a. to inform the reader about vampire bats

☐ b. to encourage the reader to protect vampire bats from hunters

☐ c. to persuade readers to kill any vampire bats they see

2. From the statements below, choose those that you believe the authors would agree with.

☐ a. All bats are dangerous to humans.

☐ b. If you are looking for vampire bats, it is best to hunt at night.

☐ c. During dry times in Central America, people probably need not fear vampire bats.

3. What do the authors imply by saying "Bats were forced out of their rural homes and into places where people lived"?

☐ a. People in rural areas are quite often attacked by bats.

☐ b. Very few people live in rural areas.

☐ c. Bats usually stay away from humans.

4. Choose the statement below that best describes the authors' position in paragraph 14.

☐ a. Most people think that the rights of vampire bats are more important than the lives of a few people or cows.

☐ b. Most people are angry when anyone tries to kill vampire bats.

☐ c. Most people would agree that the safety of humans is more important than kindness toward vampire bats.

_____ Number of correct answers

Record your personal assessment of your work on the Critical Thinking Chart on page 104.

Summarizing and Paraphrasing

Follow the directions provided for question 1. Put an X in the box next to the correct answer for the other questions.

1. Reread paragraph 5 in the article. Below, write a summary of the paragraph in no more than 25 words.

_____

_____

_____

Reread your summary and decide whether it covers the important ideas in the paragraph. Next, decide how to shorten the summary to 15 words or less without leaving out any essential information. Write this summary below.

_____

_____

_____

2. Read the statement from the article below. Then read the paraphrase of that statement. Choose the reason that best tells why the paraphrase does not say the same thing as the statement.

   Statement: Some people rub garlic on their animals to protect them against vampire bats.

   Paraphrase: To stop vampire bats from killing their animals, many people rub garlic on the bats.

☐ a. Paraphrase says too much.

☐ b. Paraphrase doesn't say enough.

☐ c. Paraphrase doesn't agree with the statement.

3. Choose the sentence that correctly restates the following sentence from the article: "Because vampire bats come out at night, their victims are usually asleep at the time of the attack."

☐ a. Most times, the victims of vampire bats are already asleep, since the bats are most active at night.

☐ b. Victims usually fall asleep as soon as the vampire bats attack them.

☐ c. Vampire bats are usually asleep when they attack their victims.

_____ Number of correct answers

Record your personal assessment of your work on the Critical Thinking Chart on page 104.

Critical Thinking

Put an X in the box next to the correct answer for questions 1, 2, 4, and 5. Follow the directions provided for question 3.

1. Which of the following statements from the article is an opinion rather than a fact?

☐ a. Vampire bats can drink their own body weight in warm blood at one meal.

☐ b. To many people, poisoning vampire bats sounds cruel.

☐ c. Slaying bats wasn't a nice job.

2. From the article, you can predict that if another serious hurricane hits Nicaragua,

☐ a. none of the people of Nicaragua will be able to sleep at night.

☐ b. vampire bats will become a serious problem again.

☐ c. farmers will kill their animals before vampire bats can attack them.

3. Reread paragraph 8. Then choose from the letters below to correctly complete the following statement. Write the letters on the lines.

According to paragraph 7, _____ happened because _____.

a. vampire bats left their caves and wells

b. caves and wells were flooded

c. vampire bats usually don't go near humans

4. If you were a parent in Central America, how could you use the information in the article to keep your family safe?

☐ a. From the article I learned that vampire bats often attack humans when bats' homes are flooded. I would keep my windows closed at night after heavy rains.

☐ b. From the article I learned that vampire bats don't like garlic. I would feed my family garlic at every meal.

☐ c. From the article I learned that vampire bats often attack at night. I would never let my family sleep at night.

5. What did you have to do to answer question 4?

☐ a. find a comparison (how things are the same)

☐ b. find a description (how something looks)

☐ c. draw a conclusion (a sensible statement based on the text and your experience)

_____ Number of correct answers

Record your personal assessment of your work on the Critical Thinking Chart on page 104.

Personal Response

I agree with the authors because _____

_____

_____

Self-Assessment

The part I found most difficult about the article was _____

_____

_____

I found this difficult because _____

_____

_____

The Man-Eating Komodo Dragon

Imagine this scene. You're walking through the Indonesian jungle with some friends. After a while, you become tired and decide to rest a bit. You sit down on a log, telling your friends to keep going. You'll catch up with them later. As you begin to relax, you suddenly realize that you're not alone. Your blood runs cold. When you turn around, you find yourself face to face with a 10-foot Komodo dragon rapidly flicking its tongue in and out. Say hello to the world's largest lizard. But do it fast. This dragon isn't here to talk.

Here, four full-grown Komodo dragons fight over a chunk of goat meat. Given the chance, any of the four would take all the meat for itself. And if there were not meat available, it would attack its fellows.

2   Luckily for you, you're not really sitting on that log. But a real person once did sit on a similar log. He was a Swiss tourist visiting the island nation of Indonesia. He grew tired of hiking and sent his friends on ahead. Later, when the tourist didn't show up, his friends went looking for him. All they found was his camera case and a bloody shirt. Everything else had been eaten by a hungry Komodo dragon.

3   Then there is the story of a father and his two adult sons. They went into the Indonesian jungle to cut some wood. The tropical heat tired them out. And the work was tedious. So the men were not particularly alert. They didn't notice the Komodo dragon sneaking up on them until it was too late. The lizard leapt at the three men. They jumped out of the way and began to run for their lives. But one of the sons got caught in a low-hanging vine. In a flash, the Komodo dragon seized him and bit off a huge chunk of his back. The father and the other son raced back and beat the lizard off. But it was too late. The son who had been attacked bled to death within an hour.

4   You may be relieved to learn that your chances of running into a Komodo dragon are pretty slim. You can find these lizards at some large zoos. Other than in these zoos, they live on only a few small islands in Indonesia. They get their name from one of these islands, Komodo. If you should happen to visit these islands, take care. Heed the warning signs along jungle paths. Pay attention when the signs say Dangerous Area or WATCH OUT: Komodo Crossing. Otherwise, you might end up in the opening paragraph of a story like this.

5   The Komodo dragon certainly looks the part of a killer. It has scaly skin, a yellow forked tongue, sharp teeth, and curved claws. It's also huge! Most Komodos are about seven feet long. A few grow to be 10 feet. Many weigh 200 pounds. Some are even bigger than that. The biggest ones probably come close to 500 pounds. It's hard to be precise, though—no one has volunteered to weigh them!

6   Komodo dragons are predators. They feed off the flesh of the animals they kill. Often they attack small creatures such as rats, goats, hens,

monkeys, and pigs. But sometimes they move up to larger prey. One of their top targets is deer. A few Komodos have killed animals as large as a horse or a water buffalo.

7   Komodos have a simple system for killing big animals. It's the same method that was used on the Indonesian woodcutter. The Komodo lunges at its prey with lightning speed. It takes a huge bite out of the victim's stomach or backside. Then it waits patiently while the poor victim bleeds to death.

8   Komodo dragons always hunt alone. They don't seem to trust each other. And they have reason to be suspicious. If a Komodo does not find anything else to eat, it is perfectly willing to feast on its fellow Komodos.

9   Komodo dragons are skillful killers. They are not fast enough, however, to run down most of their prey. They can run up to 11 miles an hour, but only for a short stretch. So they ambush their prey from behind. At times they also take to the water in search of food. Komodos are fine swimmers. They have no trouble diving or swimming through strong ocean currents.

10   Komodo dragons are terribly smart. They plan some of their meals far in advance. They do this by keeping watch on pregnant goats and horses. Komodos like to be around just after

these creatures give birth. A helpless mother and her newborn babies make a great meal.

11   Big Komodo dragons are also scavengers. They will eat the meat of animals they didn't kill. And it's not just animal meat they crave. Komodos have been found digging in cemeteries. They were trying to get at human corpses that had been buried there.

12   Clearly, Komodos will eat just about any kind of flesh they can find. They don't care if it is fresh or rotten. In fact, the smellier and more rotten the meat, the better. A strong odor just makes the food easier to find. A Komodo sniffs out rotting meat with its tongue. This tongue can detect a meal from as far away as five miles. The tongue also lets you know if the lizard considers you a good meal. The faster a Komodo flicks its tongue in and out, the tastier it thinks you will be.

13   Once a Komodo dragon finds food, it isn't shy about eating it. It will chow down its meal as fast as possible. There is a reason for the bad manners. Every Komodo wants to prevent other Komodos from stealing its goat or pig or deer. An average Komodo can bite off the hindquarter of a goat in one gulp. A 110-pound Komodo once ate a 68-pound pig in 17 minutes. Komodos can eat up to 80 percent of their body weight in one meal. If you weighed

100 pounds, you would have to eat 320 quarter-pound burgers to match that record.

14   And Komodo dragons don't waste anything. They will swallow a goat's head, *including* its horns and teeth. They will eat a porcupine, quills and all. The hooves of a horse are no problem, either. It's hard to think of any animal that is a more efficient eater.

15   The habits of a Komodo dragon might seem disgusting to you. You would not be alone in that opinion. But the Komodo dragon is a marvel of nature. It knows what it wants, and it knows how to get it. All you have to do is be sure that what it wants isn't you!

If you have been timed while reading this article, enter your reading time below. Then turn to the Words-per-Minute Table on page 101 and look up your reading speed (words per minute). Enter your reading speed on the graph on page 102.

Reading Time: Lesson 8

_____ : _____

Minutes   Seconds

A | Finding the Main Idea

One statement below expresses the main idea of the article. One statement is too general, or too broad. The other statement explains only part of the article; it is too narrow. Label the statements using the following key:

M—Main Idea   B—Too Broad   N—Too Narrow

_____ 1. Other than in large zoos, the only place where you can see Komodo dragons is on a few small islands in Indonesia.

_____ 2. Anyone traveling through the jungles of Komodo Island has a very good reason to stay alert—the Komodo dragon.

_____ 3. Beware of the Komodo dragon, a powerful lizard that is happy to eat the flesh of monkeys, rats, and human beings.

_____ Score 15 points for a correct M answer.

_____ Score 5 points for each correct B or N answer.

_____ **Total Score:** Finding the Main Idea

B | Recalling Facts

How well do you remember the facts in the article? Put an X in the box next to the answer that correctly completes each statement about the article.

1. Most Komodo dragons are about
   - [ ] a. 7 feet long.
   - [ ] b. 20 feet long.
   - [ ] c. 2 feet long.

2. Komodo dragons' favorite foods do *not* include
   - [ ] a. pigs.
   - [ ] b. rodents.
   - [ ] c. bananas.

3. Komodos have been known to keep watch on pregnant animals so that they can
   - [ ] a. eat the newborn babies and their mothers.
   - [ ] b. protect the mother and baby.
   - [ ] c. keep track of the animals in their area.

4. Komodo dragons are attracted by
   - [ ] a. bright lights.
   - [ ] b. loud noises.
   - [ ] c. strong odors.

5. After a Komodo dragon takes a big bite out of its prey, it
   - [ ] a. carries the animal back home.
   - [ ] b. waits for the animal to bleed to death.
   - [ ] c. leaves the scene and comes back much later.

Score 5 points for each correct answer.

_____ **Total Score:** Recalling Facts

C | Making Inferences

When you combine your own experience with information from a text to draw a conclusion that is not directly stated in that text, you are making an inference. Below are five statements that may or may not be inferences based on information in the article. Label the statements using the following key:

C—Correct Inference   **F—Faulty Inference**

_____ 1. The Komodo dragon is used to hot and humid weather.

_____ 2. Komodo dragons are ruthless killers that never show pity on their victims, no matter how young or helpless they are.

_____ 3. If you are on Komodo Island and want to attract a Komodo dragon, put out some rotten meat and then wait.

_____ 4. The natives of Komodo Island make good use of the body parts that a Komodo dragon leaves behind after it has eaten its prey.

_____ 5. A good way to escape from a Komodo dragon is by jumping into a river or the ocean.

Score 5 points for each correct answer.

_____ **Total Score:** Making Inferences

D | Using Words Precisely

Each numbered sentence below contains an underlined word or phrase from the article. Following the sentence are three definitions. One definition is closest to the meaning of the underlined word. One definition is opposite or nearly opposite. Label those two definitions using the following key; do not label the remaining definition.

C—Closest   **O—Opposite or Nearly Opposite**

1. And the work was <u>tedious</u>.

_____ a. exciting and fast-moving

_____ b. backbreaking

_____ c. tiresome, dull, and slow-moving

2. You may be <u>relieved</u> to learn that your chances of running into a Komodo dragon are pretty slim.

_____ a. set free from worry or pain

_____ b. worried

_____ c. excited

3. <u>Heed</u> the warning signs along jungle paths.

_____ a. read

_____ b. pay attention to

_____ c. ignore

4. But sometimes they move up to larger <u>prey</u>.

_____ a. lizards

_____ b. animals who kill other animals for food

_____ c. animals who are killed by another animal for food

5. So they <u>ambush</u> their prey from behind.

_____ a. defend

_____ b. attack without warning

_____ c. imitate

_____ Score 3 points for each correct C answer.

_____ Score 2 points for each correct O answer.

_____ **Total Score:** Using Words Precisely

Enter the four total scores in the spaces below, and add them together to find your Reading Comprehension Score. Then record your score on the graph on page 103.

Score	Question Type	Lesson 8
_____	Finding the Main Idea	
_____	Recalling Facts	
_____	Making Inferences	
_____	Using Words Precisely	
_____	**Reading Comprehension Score**	

Author's Approach

Put an X in the box next to the correct answer.

1. What is the authors' purpose in writing "The Man-Eating Komodo Dragon"?

☐ a. to encourage the reader to travel to Indonesia

☐ b. to inform the reader about a dangerous and powerful lizard

☐ c. to emphasize the similarities between Komodo dragons and other lizards

2. Which of the following statements from the article best describes the way Komodo dragons treat each other?

☐ a. If a Komodo does not find anything else to eat, it is perfectly willing to feast on its fellow Komodos.

☐ b. Komodo dragons are terribly smart. They plan some of their meals far in advance.

☐ c. Komodos have been found digging in cemeteries.

3. Judging by statements from the article "The Man-Eating Komodo Dragon," you can conclude that the authors want the reader to think that

☐ a. anyone who is killed by a Komodo dragon is simply careless.

☐ b. Komodo dragons should all be killed because they are too dangerous to humans.

☐ c. people should stay far away from wild Komodo dragons.

_____ Number of correct answers

Record your personal assessment of your work on the Critical Thinking Chart on page 104.

Summarizing and Paraphrasing

Follow the directions provided for question 1. Put an X in the box next to the correct answer for the other questions.

1. Reread paragraph 7 in the article. Below, write a summary of the paragraph in no more than 25 words.

_____

_____

_____

_____

Reread your summary and decide whether it covers the important ideas in the paragraph. Next, decide how to shorten the summary to 15 words or less without leaving out any essential information. Write this summary below.

_____

_____

_____

2. Choose the best one-sentence paraphrase for the following sentence from the article: "The faster a Komodo flicks its tongue in and out, the tastier it thinks you will be."

☐ a. If the Komodo dragon has enjoyed a meal it has eaten, it flicks its tongue in and out quickly.

☐ b. Before a meal, the Komodo dragon always flicks its tongue in and out quickly.

☐ c. When a Komodo dragon flicks its tongue in and out quickly near its victim, it is showing that it thinks the victim will be delicious.

3. Read the statement from the article below. Then read the paraphrase of that statement. Choose the reason that best tells why the paraphrase does not say the same thing as the statement.

Statement: The Komodo uses its tongue to sniff out rotting meat from as far away as five miles.

Paraphrase: The Komodo can smell meat from a distance of five miles.

☐ a. Paraphrase says too much.

☐ b. Paraphrase doesn't say enough.

☐ c. Paraphrase doesn't agree with the statement.

_____ Number of correct answers

Record your personal assessment of your work on the Critical Thinking Chart on page 104.

Critical Thinking

Follow the directions provided for questions 1, 3, and 4. Put an X in the box next to the correct answer for the other questions.

1. For each statement below, write O if it expresses an opinion or write F if it expresses a fact.

_____ a. A 110-pound Komodo once ate a 68-pound pig in 17 minutes.

_____ b. But the Komodo dragon is a marvel of nature.

_____ c. It [the Komodo dragon] has scaly skin, a yellow forked tongue, sharp teeth, and curved claws.

CRITICAL THINKING

2. From what the article told about what happened to the Swiss tourist, you can predict that

☐ a. tourists who have heard the story will watch out for Komodo dragons.

☐ b. no one else will ever walk through the Indonesian jungle again.

☐ c. no one will visit Indonesia on vacation anymore.

3. Choose from the letters below to correctly complete the following statement. Write the letters on the lines.

On the positive side, _____, but on the negative side _____.

a. the Komodo dragon can grow to be 10 feet long

b. the Komodo dragon is well suited to its home

c. the Komodo dragon sometimes hunts humans

4. Reread paragraph 13. Then choose from the letters below to correctly complete the following statement. Write the letters on the lines.

According to paragraph 13, _____ because _____.

a. Komodos want to prevent other Komodos from eating their prey

b. a 110-pound Komodo once ate a 68-pound pig

c. Komodo dragons eat quickly

5. What did you have to do to answer question 4?

☐ a. find a cause (why something happened)

☐ b. find a comparison (how things are the same)

☐ c. find an opinion (what someone thinks about something)

_____ Number of correct answers

Record your personal assessment of your work on the Critical Thinking Chart on page 104.

Personal Response

What was most surprising or interesting to you about this article?

_____

_____

_____

_____

Self-Assessment

When reading the article, I was having trouble with _____

_____

_____

_____

_____

Elephant on the Rampage

Kathy Lawler thought it sounded like fun. Her children, eight-year-old Lauren and three-year-old C. J., couldn't wait to do it. So Lawler paid for them all to have a ride on a circus elephant. The Lawlers hoped to get a nice, gentle ride. Instead they got the ride of their lives.

2   It was almost 5 o'clock in the evening on February 1, 1992. The Great American Circus was about to start in Palm Bay, Florida. First, though, people in the crowd could take elephant rides. Lawler and her children climbed onto an Indian elephant named Kelly. They sat in a metal basket on her back. Three other children also climbed on.

Elephants are usually intelligent, gentle, and sociable animals. However, an elephant that is mistreated or kept in a small space can lose its patient and agreeable nature. Then watch out!

3   Kelly was a circus pro. She had been giving rides for more than 10 years. She always moved slowly, walking next to a metal fence inside the ring. Lawler thought Kelly looked very tame. Her stride seemed firm and steady. As the ride began, C. J. and the other children screamed with delight.

4   Then it happened. "About two-thirds of the way around the ring, Kelly smashed into [the fence]," Lawler later recalled. "And I thought, 'Well, she's a little testy today. I'll be glad when this ride is over.'" Lawler didn't know it, but the "ride" was just beginning.

5   Kelly backed off and rammed the fence again. Her trainer hurried to stop her. Using his training hook, he tried to turn Kelly away from the fence. But that just made the 8,000-pound animal madder. Kelly picked up her trainer with her trunk and hurled him across the ring like a rag doll. The children on Kelly's back kept screaming—but now their screams were from sheer terror.

6   The trainer got back on his feet. Again, he tried to control Kelly. But again, he failed. By this time, the elephant had broken through the fence. She charged toward the bleachers, where more than 2,000 people watched in shock. They knew that *this* wasn't part of the act. In panic, people scrambled over each other to reach the exits. An announcer's voice asked everyone to stay calm, but no one paid any attention to this request.

7   Then, suddenly, Kelly turned away from the bleachers. She reached up with her trunk and began to rip at the cables and wires that held up the tent. Sparks flew in all directions. A metal beam broke loose. It nearly hit Lawler and the five children, who were still on the elephant's back.

8   Meanwhile, another circus worker rushed to help. He climbed onto an elephant named Irene. He thought that if he could get Irene close to Kelly, he could grab the children out of the basket. As Irene moved in, Kathy Lawler picked up C. J. She leaned out of the basket and handed her son to the man on Irene's back. Somehow, though, C. J. slipped out of the man's hands. The boy landed on the ground a few feet from Kelly's stamping feet.

9   "Get my kid!" yelled Lawler.

10 Luckily, someone rushed in and dragged C. J. to safety. Before Lawler could hand over any other children, though, Kelly knocked Irene out of the way. She went charging out of the tent and began to attack a car parked

nearby. At that point, Police Officer Blayne Doyle came to the rescue. Doyle had been directing traffic outside the tent. He saw the elephant smash the car with her head and trunk. "She was very mad," Doyle said later.

11   Doyle ran up to the crazed beast. "Hand me one of the kids!" he shouted to Lawler.

12   But Kelly was too quick for him. She whirled her trunk around and knocked Doyle to the ground. Doyle scrambled to his feet. Once again he tried to get close to the elephant. This time Kelly grabbed him and pushed him face down in front of her.

13   Kathy Lawler watched in horror as the great creature tried to crush Doyle beneath her massive front legs. Doyle thought he had seen everything in his 22 years on the police force. But this was his closest brush with death. He could barely breathe. He could feel Kelly crushing the life out of him. "In my lifetime," he later said, "I've been shot. I've been stabbed. I've wrecked police cars and police motorcycles. I've been in an airplane crash. But I've never been as scared as I was underneath that elephant."

14   Fortunately, a circus worker managed to distract Kelly by waving a training hook in front of her face. For a few seconds, she stopped her attack on Doyle. That was just long enough for someone else to dart in and pull Doyle away. Kelly, however, was still furious. She turned back to the car and banged at it some more. She didn't even notice the person who came close enough to reach up to the basket. Lawler handed down a child safely.

15   A moment later, Irene and her trainer came alongside again. Lawler managed to hand the three remaining children, one by one, to the trainer. Then Lawler herself jumped onto Irene's back.

16   The drama was over for Kathy Lawler and the five frightened children. But it wasn't over for Kelly. Still as mad as ever, she moved on to attack a truck. She smashed in its side and ripped off a door. The truck's jagged metal cut the elephant's trunk, causing it to bleed.

17   Nothing could calm Kelly down. Her trainer knew what had to be done. "You're going to have to kill that elephant," he told Officer Doyle. "She's going to kill someone if you don't."

18   Doyle didn't want to shoot Kelly. "I love animals," he said later. He would have used a tranquilizer gun if he'd had one. That would have knocked Kelly out without killing her. But Doyle had only his regular gun. He hesitated a moment. But Kelly gave him no choice. She charged back toward the circus tent. There were still people inside. Doyle knew he now had to shoot to kill.

19   Doyle ran beside Kelly, firing his pistol into the elephant's ear. Two other officers also opened fire. Wounded, but not slowed down, Kelly tore into the bleachers. The officers had to stop shooting. They did not want to hit anyone. They tried to direct people out of the tent. "Everyone was screaming and running," Doyle said. Then, with another sudden movement, Kelly turned and bolted out of the tent. Here, at last, an officer with a high-powered rifle killed her.

20   Doyle knew he had done his job. Still, he felt terrible. "I went over behind the wall and cried," he said. "We had to destroy one of God's most beautiful creatures."

If you have been timed while reading this article, enter your reading time below. Then turn to the Words-per-Minute Table on page 101 and look up your reading speed (words per minute). Enter your reading speed on the graph on page 102.

Reading Time: Lesson 9

_____ : _____
Minutes   Seconds

A Finding the Main Idea

One statement below expresses the main idea of the article. One statement is too general, or too broad. The other statement explains only part of the article; it is too narrow. Label the statements using the following key:

M—Main Idea   **B—Too Broad**   **N—Too Narrow**

_____ 1. When a usually calm circus elephant suddenly ran wild, she terrified her riders and others, and had to be killed.

_____ 2. Kathy Lawler tried to get her son off an elephant that had gone wild, but he fell to the ground and was almost stepped on by the beast.

_____ 3. During the many years in which elephants have given circus customers rides, there have been few rides as exciting as the one Kathy Lawler had.

_____ Score 15 points for a correct M answer.

_____ Score 5 points for each correct B or N answer.

_____ **Total Score:** Finding the Main Idea

B Recalling Facts

How well do you remember the facts in the article? Put an X in the box next to the answer that correctly completes each statement about the article.

1. Kathy Lawler rode the elephant with her
   ☐ a. five children.
   ☐ b. two children and five others.
   ☐ c. two children and three others.

2. The elephant, Kelly, went wild
   ☐ a. for no known reason.
   ☐ b. because of a sudden loud noise.
   ☐ c. when her trainer beat her.

3. When Kathy tried to hand a child down to Officer Doyle, the elephant
   ☐ a. grabbed the child with her trunk.
   ☐ b. used her trunk to knock down the officer.
   ☐ c. shook so hard that Kathy dropped the child.

4. A circus worker saved Officer Doyle from Kelly by
   ☐ a. calming the elephant down for a minute.
   ☐ b. getting the elephant's attention briefly.
   ☐ c. bringing another elephant to bump Kelly away from the downed officer.

5. Kelly's wild behavior ended when
   ☐ a. an officer with a powerful rifle killed her.
   ☐ b. her trainer gave her her favorite foods.
   ☐ c. Officer Doyle shot her with his pistol.

Score 5 points for each correct answer.

_____ **Total Score:** Recalling Facts

C | Making Inferences

When you combine your own experience with information from a text to draw a conclusion that is not directly stated in that text, you are making an inference. Below are five statements that may or may not be inferences based on information in the article. Label the statements using the following key:

C—Correct Inference   **F—Faulty Inference**

_____ 1. Officer Doyle disliked and feared elephants.

_____ 2. At least until this wild ride, Kathy Lawler enjoyed trying unusual experiences.

_____ 3. The animal trainer who trained Kelly did a poor job.

_____ 4. An experience such as Kelly's rampage never happened before at a circus and will never happen again.

_____ 5. Officer Doyle would agree that more people should have opportunities to see elephants under well-supervised conditions.

Score 5 points for each correct answer.

_____ **Total Score:** Making Inferences

D | Using Words Precisely

Each numbered sentence below contains an underlined word or phrase from the article. Following the sentence are three definitions. One definition is closest to the meaning of the underlined word. One definition is opposite or nearly opposite. Label those two definitions using the following key; do not label the remaining definition.

C—Closest   **O—Opposite or Nearly Opposite**

1. Kelly picked up her trainer and <u>hurled</u> him across the ring like a rag doll.

_____ a. threw

_____ b. photographed

_____ c. caught

2. The truck's <u>jagged</u> metal cut the elephant's trunk.

_____ a. uneven

_____ b. dirty

_____ c. smooth

3. An announcer's voice asked everyone to stay calm, but no one paid any attention to this <u>request</u>.

_____ a. idea

_____ b. plea; appeal

_____ c. demand

4. Fortunately, a circus worker managed to <u>distract Kelly</u> by waving a training hook in front of her face.

_____ a. improve Kelly's ability to concentrate

_____ b. get Kelly's attention

_____ c. injure Kelly

5. That was just long enough for someone to <u>dart</u> in and pull Doyle away.

_____ a. follow

_____ b. dawdle

_____ c. rush

_____ Score 3 points for each correct C answer.

_____ Score 2 points for each correct O answer.

_____ **Total Score:** Using Words Precisely

Enter the four total scores in the spaces below, and add them together to find your Reading Comprehension Score. Then record your score on the graph on page 103.

Score	Question Type	Lesson 9
_____	Finding the Main Idea	
_____	Recalling Facts	
_____	Making Inferences	
_____	Using Words Precisely	
_____	**Reading Comprehension Score**	

Author's Approach

Put an X in the box next to the correct answer.

1. What do the authors mean by the statement "As the ride began, C.J. and the other children screamed with delight"?

☐ a. The children were trying to act happy, but they were really frightened.

☐ b. The children screamed because they were surprised that the ride had begun.

☐ c. The children were excited and happy.

2. From the statements below, choose those that you believe the authors would agree with.

☐ a. Some people are willing to put themselves in danger to save others.

☐ b. Kelly's trainer didn't know anything about training elephants.

☐ c. Sometimes the only way to stop an elephant is to kill it.

3. Choose the statement below that is the weakest argument for taking a ride on an elephant.

☐ a. Elephant rides are fun.

☐ b. Riding on an elephant can be dangerous.

☐ c. Riding on an elephant is a memorable experience.

_____ Number of correct answers

Record your personal assessment of your work on the Critical Thinking Chart on page 104.

Summarizing and Paraphrasing

Follow the directions provided for question 1. Put an X in the box next to the correct answer for the other questions.

1. Complete the following one-sentence summary of the article using the lettered phrases from the phrase bank below. Write the letters on the lines.

Phrase Bank

a. Kathy Lawler's decision to ride the elephant with her children

b. the death of the elephant

c. how the elephant went out of control

The article "Elephant on the Rampage" begins with _____, goes on to explain _____, and ends with _____.

2. Read the statement from the article below. Then read the paraphrase of that statement. Choose the reason that best tells why the paraphrase does not say the same thing as the statement.

Statement: Someone distracted Kelly by waving a training hook in front of her face, allowing Doyle to escape.

Paraphrase: Kelly was distracted for a moment by Doyle, who waved a training hook in front of her face.

☐ a. Paraphrase says too much.

☐ b. Paraphrase doesn't say enough.

☐ c. Paraphrase doesn't agree with the statement.

3. Choose the best one-sentence paraphrase for the following sentence from the article: "An announcer's voice asked everyone to stay calm, but no one paid any attention to this request."

☐ a. No one could hear the announcer's voice, asking everyone to stay calm.

☐ b. People were panicking, even though the announcer asked them to stay calm.

☐ c. The announcer's calm voice was able to keep the people from panicking.

_____ Number of correct answers

Record your personal assessment of your work on the Critical Thinking Chart on page 104.

Critical Thinking

Put an X in the box next to the correct answer for questions 1, 3, and 4. Follow the directions provided for the other questions.

1. From what Officer Doyle said after the elephant died, you can predict that

☐ a. he will feel bad about the elephant's death for a while.

☐ b. he will be angry with the officer who finally shot the elephant.

☐ c. he will be afraid of any elephant he sees from now on.

2. Choose from the letters below to correctly complete the following statement. Write the letters on the lines.

On the positive side, _____, but on the negative side _____.

   a. Kelly had to be killed

   b. Kelly was a circus pro

   c. Kelly was finally stopped

3. What was the effect of Kelly's rampage on the children?

☐ a. They were delighted.

☐ b. They became terrified.

☐ c. They became bored and irritable.

4. Of the following theme categories, which would this story fit into?

☐ a. People and animals should stay away from each other as much as possible.

☐ b. Animals can sometimes lose control.

☐ c. People should never rely on animals.

5. In which paragraph did you find your information or details to answer question 2?_____

_____ Number of correct answers

Record your personal assessment of your work on the Critical Thinking Chart on page 104.

Personal Response

I wonder why _____

_____

_____

_____

_____

Self-Assessment

A word or phrase in the article that I do not understand is _____

_____

_____

_____

_____

Tigers: Humans on the Menu

Quiz time: Which is more dangerous to humans—a healthy tiger or an injured tiger?

2   The answer is the injured tiger. Most healthy tigers want nothing to do with people. They're too busy chasing down deer and wild hogs. But what about a disabled tiger? What if it can no longer catch its natural prey? Imagine this tiger wandering through the fields. Think of its stomach rumbling with hunger. What do you guess it would do if it came upon a human being?

3   That was what happened in a remote part of Nepal in December 1979.

The tiger is the largest member of the cat family. A healthy tiger normally feeds on large prey such as deer, antelope, and wild pigs. A sick or injured tiger may find it easier to attack slow-moving humans. Some tigers even develop a taste for humans.

There, a schoolteacher left his hut as he did every morning. He headed toward the river to wash up. This man wasn't the only one going to the river that day. A second man was walking about 50 yards behind the schoolteacher.

4   Meanwhile, a three-year-old tiger padded along the water's edge. The tiger walked slowly, with a deep limp. For the past year it had been unable to hunt its usual prey. A fight with another tiger had left it with a bad front leg. No longer could it chase down a fleet-footed deer. No longer could it take on a small elephant. It could not even manage to kill a wild pig.

5   To survive, the tiger had turned to farm animals. It had started to kill and eat cattle. It had also learned to eat the water buffaloes that local farmers kept. Its new diet brought it closer and closer to the village, closer and closer to people.

6   That morning, the schoolteacher climbed the steep bank to the river. When he reached the top, he found himself face-to-face with the injured tiger. For a moment, neither one moved. Then the tiger pounced and the schoolteacher screamed. The man

who had been 50 yards back hurried forward. He saw the schoolteacher trying to ward off the tiger. But it was no use. With a few swipes of its claws, the tiger ripped through the school-teacher's clothes. The tiger's teeth tore into the teacher's body. Within seconds, the schoolteacher was dead.

7   The people in the village were shocked when they heard the news. Still, it was not the first time a tiger had attacked a person. In fact, tigers have killed thousands of people. From India to China to Vietnam, these beasts are known to be deadly to human beings.

8   Most man-eating tigers are old or disabled. Like the one that killed the schoolteacher, they can't catch wild prey. People in India saw this back in the 1930s. Villagers were terrorized by not one man-eating tiger, but 16. Slowly, these tigers were rounded up. All were found to have some kind of injury. Many had gunshot wounds. The rest had wounds caused by porcupine quills.

9   Sometimes, though, healthy tigers become man-eaters. This may happen when there is a shortage of wild prey in the region. Or it may happen by

accident. If someone surprises a tiger, the animal may attack. Experts think that's what happened to Mahesh Howard. Howard was a grasscutter in India. One day in 1982 he went into the jungle. He must have come too close to a tiger's den. When Howard did not return, search parties went to look for him. They found his blood-stained clothes and six of his bones, stripped clean of flesh. In the mud next to these remains were the pawprints of a large tiger.

10 It was bad enough that Mahesh Howard had been killed and eaten. But his death was not the only sad part of the story. The tiger that killed him found that it liked the taste of human flesh. As one tiger expert says, "When an animal has killed and eaten a person, the danger is that it will add men to its menu."

11 And so it was in this case. In 1985 another grasscutter was in the same region. This man's name was Sudebar Ali. As Ali worked, he noticed a strange silence. There were no birds chirping, no monkeys chattering. Ali didn't know it, but he was being stalked by a tiger. Suddenly, the creature leaped out at him. Grabbing Ali's neck in its mouth, the tiger threw him into the air. Then it pounced on him, pinning him to the ground. The tiger bit through Ali's hand and raked its claws across his face. Luckily, a friend was nearby. The friend managed to distract the tiger while Ali escaped to safety. By the pawprints that the tiger left, game wardens knew that this tiger was the same one that had killed Mahesh Howard.

12 Tigers don't always have to kill people to acquire a taste for human flesh. In wartime, the bodies of dead soldiers may be left on the jungle floor. Tigers may start to feast on these bodies. That happened in World War II and again during the Vietnam War. In Vietnam, the tigers grew especially bold. They began to go after live soldiers. One tiger grabbed a U.S. marine right out of his foxhole. The man lived only because the tiger tried to drag him under a barbed wire fence. The marine got caught in the wire. That gave his fellow soldiers time to run over and drive the tiger off.

13 Researchers say there are other ways for tigers to learn to eat humans. One researcher thinks some may learn by watching their mothers. He says, "Females become man-eaters and teach their young to be man-eaters. [In time,] there is a whole crew of healthy man-eaters." Another researcher thinks salty water might be to blame. He believes high salt levels in drinking water may change a tiger's mood. That would explain why so many tigers in Bangladesh are man-eaters. There is not much fresh water there. The tigers must drink from the sea. Could that be why they are the most fearless and aggressive tigers in the world?

14 Humans may never figure out all the reasons why one tiger turns away and another pounces. One expert says that only a single tiger in 100 is a hard-core man-eater. That means only one in 100 will seek out human prey. But one in three will attack a human that crosses its path. Given this fact, many people fear tiger attacks will increase. After all, each year humans move deeper and deeper into the jungle. And as one Indian farmer says, it seems that "tigers and people cannot share space."

If you have been timed while reading this article, enter your reading time below. Then turn to the Words-per-Minute Table on page 101 and look up your reading speed (words per minute). Enter your reading speed on the graph on page 102.

Reading Time: Lesson 10

———— : ————
Minutes   Seconds

A Finding the Main Idea

One statement below expresses the main idea of the article. One statement is too general, or too broad. The other statement explains only part of the article; it is too narrow. Label the statements using the following key:

M—Main Idea   **B—Too Broad**   **N—Too Narrow**

_____ 1. As people move into the jungles of the world, they have more problems with wild animals.

_____ 2. There are, unfortunately, many causes that turn tigers into man-eaters.

_____ 3. Some female tigers become man-eaters and teach their young to be man-eaters.

_____ Score 15 points for a correct M answer.

_____ Score 5 points for each correct B or N answer.

_____ **Total Score:** Finding the Main Idea

B Recalling Facts

How well do you remember the facts in the article? Put an X in the box next to the answer that correctly completes each statement about the article.

1. An injured tiger is dangerous to people because it
   ☐ a. feels grumpy.
   ☐ b. is hungry.
   ☐ c. goes crazy.

2. Tigers are regularly a threat to human beings in
   ☐ a. India, China, and Vietnam.
   ☐ b. Nepal, Alaska, and India.
   ☐ c. Asia and Europe.

3. In one case in India in the 1930s, several tigers were made man-eaters by
   ☐ a. porcupine quill injuries.
   ☐ b. the teaching of their mother tiger.
   ☐ c. high levels of salt in their diet.

4. After a tiger kills a human being, it
   ☐ a. eats everything, including clothes.
   ☐ b. usually leaves the dead body alone.
   ☐ c. may develop a taste for human flesh.

5. The tigers that become hard-core man-eaters are
   ☐ a. about one in a hundred.
   ☐ b. about one in three.
   ☐ c. usually females.

Score 5 points for each correct answer.

_____ **Total Score:** Recalling Facts

C Making Inferences

When you combine your own experience with information from a text to draw a conclusion that is not directly stated in that text, you are making an inference. Below are five statements that may or may not be inferences based on information in the article. Label the statements using the following key:

C—Correct Inference   F—Faulty Inference

_____ 1. It is not unusual for people in Nepal to live in small houses without running water.

_____ 2. A careless hunter who wounds a tiger but does not kill it may create a man-eater.

_____ 3. Every tiger has pawprints that belong to it alone.

_____ 4. Because tigers are not native to North America, no Americans have been attacked by tigers.

_____ 5. Mother tigers teach their babies how to take care of themselves before the young tigers go off on their own.

Score 5 points for each correct answer.

_____ **Total Score:** Making Inferences

D Using Words Precisely

Each numbered sentence below contains an underlined word or phrase from the article. Following the sentence are three definitions. One definition is closest to the meaning of the underlined word. One definition is opposite or nearly opposite. Label those two definitions using the following key; do not label the remaining definition.

C—Closest   O—Opposite or Nearly Opposite

1. No longer could it chase down a <u>fleet</u>-footed deer.

_____ a. quick

_____ b. slow

_____ c. brown

2. He saw the schoolteacher trying to <u>ward off</u> the tiger.

_____ a. run from

_____ b. submit to

_____ c. resist

3. Tigers may start to <u>feast</u> on these bodies.

_____ a. go hungry

_____ b. stuff themselves

_____ c. lie down

4. Could that be why they are the most fearless and <u>aggressive</u> tigers in the world?

_____ a. friendly

_____ b. colorful

_____ c. willing to fight

5. That means only one in 100 will <u>seek out</u> human prey.

_____ a. limit oneself to

_____ b. look for; hunt for

_____ c. avoid; ignore

_____ Score 3 points for each correct C answer.

_____ Score 2 points for each correct O answer.

_____ **Total Score:** Using Words Precisely

Enter the four total scores in the spaces below, and add them together to find your Reading Comprehension Score. Then record your score on the graph on page 103.

Score	Question Type	Lesson 10
_____	Finding the Main Idea	
_____	Recalling Facts	
_____	Making Inferences	
_____	Using Words Precisely	
_____	**Reading Comprehension Score**	

Author's Approach

Put an X in the box next to the correct answer.

1. The authors use the first sentence of the article to

☐ a. describe the qualities of tigers.

☐ b. compare healthy tigers and injured tigers.

☐ c. introduce the topic of the article.

2. What is the authors' purpose in writing "Tigers: Humans on the Menu"?

☐ a. to persuade the reader to save endangered species

☐ b. to inform the reader about man-eating tigers

☐ c. to express an opinion about tigers

3. Judging by statements from the article "Tigers: Humans on the Menu," you can conclude that the authors want the reader to think that

☐ a. tigers are efficient killers.

☐ b. most tigers enjoy eating humans more than they enjoy eating other animals.

☐ c. tigers are the most dangerous animals in the world.

4. The authors tell this story mainly by

☐ a. retelling personal experiences.

☐ b. comparing different topics.

☐ c. telling different stories about the same topic.

_____ Number of correct answers

Record your personal assessment of your work on the Critical Thinking Chart on page 104.

Summarizing and Paraphrasing

Put an X in the box next to the correct answer for question 1. Follow the directions provided for question 2.

1. Below are summaries of the article. Choose the summary that says all the most important things about the article but in the fewest words.

☐ a. Many people have been killed by man-eating tigers that are unable or unwilling to hunt for their usual prey. Although man-eating tigers are rare now, their numbers may increase as humans move deeper into the jungles.

☐ b. When a schoolteacher in Nepal came face-to-face with an injured tiger, the teacher never had a chance. The tiger killed him quickly. People in the village were shocked but not surprised, since tigers had killed humans before.

☐ c. Tigers become man-eaters for many reasons. Some tigers get a taste for human flesh during wartime when human bodies are left on the jungle floor after a battle.

2. Reread paragraph 4 in the article. Below, write a summary of the paragraph in no more than 25 words.

_____

_____

_____

_____

Reread your summary and decide whether it covers the important ideas in the paragraph. Next, decide how to shorten the summary to 15 words or less without leaving out any essential information. Write this summary below.

_____

_____

_____

_____ Number of correct answers

Record your personal assessment of your work on the Critical Thinking Chart on page 104.

Critical Thinking

Follow the directions provided for questions 1, 3, and 5. Put an X in the box next to the correct answer for the other questions.

1. For each statement below, write O if it expresses an opinion or write F if it expresses a fact.

_____ a. There are too many tigers in the world today.

_____ b. During the 1930s Indians discovered that many tigers who began eating humans had been injured.

_____ c. The theory that tigers become man-eaters because the water they drink is too salty makes no sense at all.

2. From the information in paragraph 14, you can predict that

☐ a. we have seen the last of the attacks by man-eating tigers.

☐ b. people will continue to be attacked by man-eating tigers.

☐ c. attacks by man-eating tigers will slow down and soon stop.

3. Choose from the letters below to correctly complete the following statement. Write the letters on the lines.

In the article _____ and _____ are different.

a. the fate of Mahesh Howard

b. the fate of the U.S. marine who was grabbed by a tiger

c. the fate of Sudebar Ali

4. What was probably the cause of the tiger's attack on grasscutter Mahesh Howard?

☐ a. The tiger had seen its mother kill and eat a man and had developed a taste for humans itself.

☐ b. The tiger was injured and couldn't hunt its regular prey.

☐ c. Mahesh had surprised the tiger with his grasscutting.

5. In which paragraph did you find your information or details to answer question 4? _____

_____ Number of correct answers

Record your personal assessment of your work on the Critical Thinking Chart on page 104.

Personal Response

If you could ask the authors of the article one question, what would it be?

_____

_____

_____

_____

Self-Assessment

One of the things I did best when reading this article was _____

_____

_____

_____

I believe I did this well because _____

_____

_____

_____

_____

Compare and Contrast

Think about the articles you have read in Unit Two. Pick the three articles that taught you the most about animal behavior. Write the titles of the articles in the first column of the chart below. Use information you learned from the articles to fill in the empty boxes in the chart.

Title	Name one new fact about the angry animal that you learned from the article.	Which facts about this animal had you known before reading the article?	What else would you like to know about the animal in the article?

If I had to choose one animal to research more thoroughly, it would be _____ because _____

_____

_____

_____

Words-per-Minute Table

Unit Two

Directions: If you were timed while reading an article, refer to the Reading Time you recorded in the box at the end of the article. Use this Words-per-Minute Table to determine your reading speed for that article. Then plot your reading speed on the graph on page 102.

Lesson / No. of Words	6 / 1,084	7 / 1,047	8 / 1,075	9 / 1,110	10 / 1,080	Seconds
1:30	723	698	717	740	720	90
1:40	650	628	645	666	648	100
1:50	591	571	586	605	589	110
2:00	542	524	538	555	540	120
2:10	500	483	496	512	498	130
2:20	465	449	461	476	463	140
2:30	434	419	430	444	432	150
2:40	407	393	403	416	405	160
2:50	383	370	379	392	381	170
3:00	361	349	358	370	360	180
3:10	342	331	339	351	341	190
3:20	325	314	323	333	324	200
3:30	310	299	307	317	309	210
3:40	296	286	293	303	295	220
3:50	283	273	280	290	282	230
4:00	271	262	269	278	270	240
4:10	260	251	258	266	259	250
4:20	250	242	248	256	249	260
4:30	241	233	239	247	240	270
4:40	232	224	230	238	231	280
4:50	224	217	222	230	223	290
5:00	217	209	215	222	216	300
5:10	210	203	208	215	209	310
5:20	203	196	202	208	203	320
5:30	197	190	195	740	196	330
5:40	191	185	190	196	191	340
5:50	186	179	184	190	185	350
6:00	181	175	179	185	180	360
6:10	176	170	174	180	175	370
6:20	171	165	170	666	171	380
6:30	167	161	165	171	166	390
6:40	163	157	161	167	165	400
6:50	159	153	157	162	158	410
7:00	155	150	154	159	154	420
7:10	151	146	150	155	151	430
7:20	148	143	147	151	147	440
7:30	145	140	143	148	144	450
7:40	141	137	140	145	141	460
7:50	138	134	137	142	138	470
8:00	136	131	134	139	135	480

Minutes and Seconds

Seconds

Plotting Your Progress: Reading Speed

Unit Two

Directions: If you were timed while reading an article, write your words-per-minute rate for that article in the box under the number of the lesson. Then plot your reading speed on the graph by putting a small X on the line directly above the number of the lesson, across from the number of words per minute you read. As you mark your speed for each lesson, graph your progress by drawing a line to connect the X's.

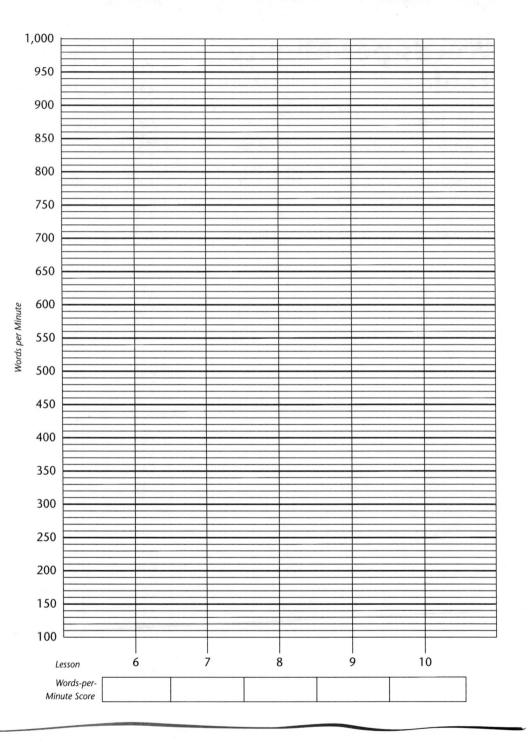

Plotting Your Progress: Reading Comprehension

Unit Two

Directions: Write your Reading Comprehension Score for each lesson in the box under the number of the lesson. Then plot your score on the graph by putting a small X on the line directly above the number of the lesson and across from the score you earned. As you mark your score for each lesson, graph your progress by drawing a line to connect the X's.

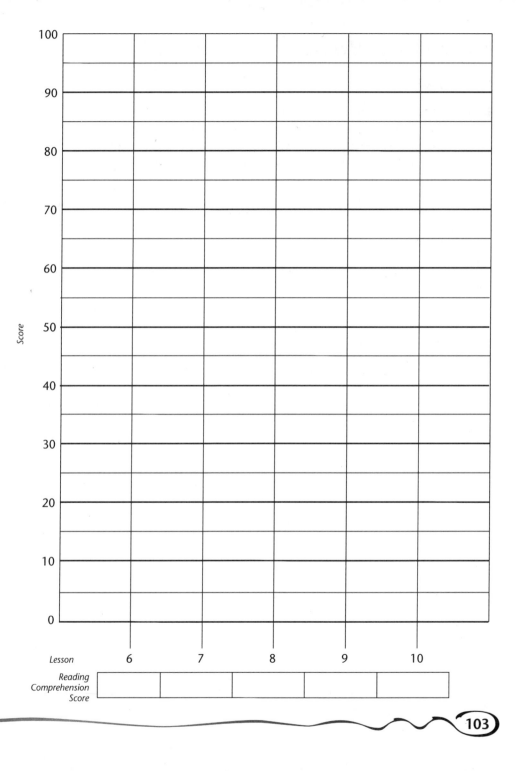

Score

Lesson	6	7	8	9	10
Reading Comprehension Score					

Plotting Your Progress: Critical Thinking

Unit Two

Directions: Work with your teacher to evaluate your responses to the Critical Thinking questions for each lesson. Then fill in the appropriate spaces in the chart below. For each lesson and each type of Critical Thinking question, do the following: Mark a minus sign (–) in the box to indicate areas in which you feel you could improve. Mark a plus sign (+) to indicate areas in which you feel you did well. Mark a minus-slash-plus sign (–/+) to indicate areas in which you had mixed success. Then write any comments you have about your performance, including ideas for improvement.

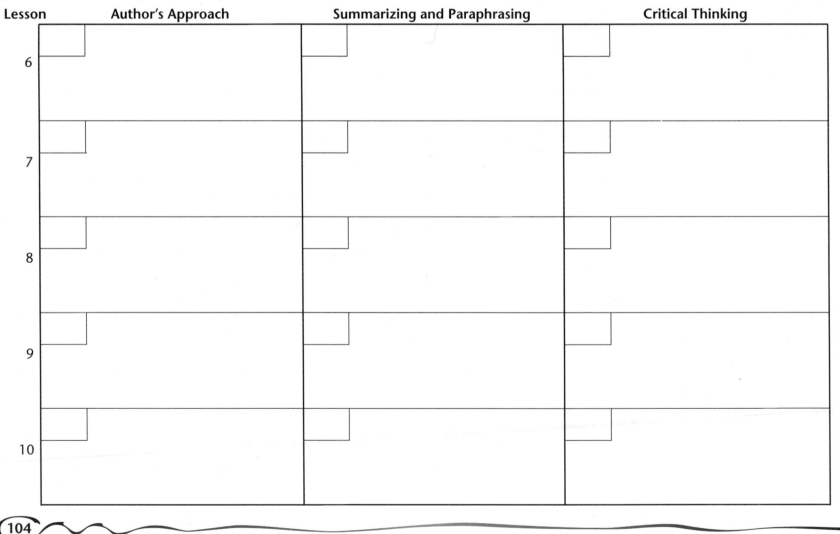

Lesson	Author's Approach	Summarizing and Paraphrasing	Critical Thinking
6			
7			
8			
9			
10			

UNIT THREE

Crocodiles: The Jaws of Death

The crocodile glided through the water without a sound. Closer and closer it came. The young woman standing in the Daintree River did not suspect a thing. She was just cooling off during a picnic in the lovely Australian wilderness.

2   The crocodile stayed below the surface of the water as it approached. It swam quickly, smoothly. Then, in one explosive burst, it opened its jaws and sank its teeth deep into the woman's flesh. The woman, whose name was Beryl Wruck, was never seen again. She another victim of Australia's deadly crocodiles. Since the late 1970s,

It isn't hard to believe that this animal is dangerous, is it? The crocodile has many, many teeth, which it uses to grab its victims and pull them deep underwater.

these crocodiles have killed and eaten at least eight people.

3   Crocodiles look dangerous—and they are! At least three kinds are known to prey on human beings. First there is the saltwater crocodile, or "saltie." This was the kind that got Beryl Wruck. Found in Australia and parts of Asia, the saltie can grow to 28 feet. It may weigh more than 4,000 pounds. A second deadly crocodile is the mugger. It, too, lives in Asia. Finally, there is the Nile crocodile, which lives along the banks of the mighty Nile River in Africa.

4   Although salties are the biggest of the three, you would not want to mess with any of these crocs. They are ferocious killers. If you wander into their territory, they won't think twice about eating you. To them, you're just another meal.

5   Crocodiles have been around since the time of the dinosaurs. They have lived in warm swamps and rivers for about 100 million years. During that time, they haven't changed much— they haven't needed to. They are among nature's most perfectly designed killing and eating machines.

6   A crocodile's body is long and flat, with rough, scaly skin. When it lies in the water, it looks like a floating log. But look again. You may see its nostrils and ears resting just above the water's surface. You may see two yellow eyes staring at you, waiting for you to come just a little closer. A crocodile's mouth is filled with about 70 razor-sharp teeth. Its jaws are so strong that no creature on earth can pry them open once they have clamped shut.

7   With all those teeth, you might think a crocodile chews its victims to pieces. But it doesn't. In fact, crocodiles don't chew at all. A crocodile simply uses its teeth and jaws to grab onto its victim. Then it goes into a "death roll." Around and around it twirls, down through the water in a corkscrew spin. The idea is to confuse the prey. When at last the crocodile stops rolling, it holds its victim underwater. Usually the dazed victim drowns within a few minutes. But crocodiles don't mind if it takes longer. Crocs can hold their breath for up to one hour. Once the prey is dead, a crocodile pulls the dead body apart, swallowing the pieces in big gulps.

8   Hilton Graham is one of the lucky few to survive a crocodile attack. In 1979 Graham was boating in northern Australia. As he stepped ashore, a crocodile shot out of the water. Its jaws locked around Graham's waist. Thirteen-year-old Peta Lynn Mann saw what was happening. She grabbed Graham's hand and tried to pull him free.

9   The crocodile was too strong for Mann, however. It dragged both her and Graham into the water. Then, for some reason, the crocodile paused a moment. Perhaps it wanted to get a better grip on Graham's body. In any case, it loosened its hold just long enough for young Mann to pull Graham to safety. Although Graham lived, he was badly hurt. His arm was crushed. He had internal injuries. And his back was riddled with teethmarks the size of golf balls.

10   It isn't very often that a crocodile will open its jaws as one did for Hilton Graham. Usually a crocodile is relentless in its attack. Crocodiles don't need to eat very often. They can go six months or more without food. Once they select a victim, though, they are reluctant to let it get away. Crocodiles have been known to jump several feet out of the water to get a meal. If necessary, they will even climb a tree to reach their prey.

11   Sandy Rossi knows how hard it is to get away from a hungry crocodile. In 1993 Rossi was serving as tutor and nanny to two American children in Zaire, Africa. On the afternoon of March 3, Rossi and the children were at the Epulu River. A friend was also there. As Rossi stood in the muddy water, a crocodile slid toward her. It grabbed her with such force that she was knocked over. She felt a sharp pain in her left arm. With a wave of horror, she realized she was caught in the jaws of a crocodile.

12   Rossi managed to call out to her friend. Then she was dragged underwater. The death roll began. Over and over Rossi tumbled as the crocodile pulled her down. She felt the bones in her upper arm snapping. Her lungs burned, aching for fresh oxygen. When the death roll stopped, Rossi summoned all her strength. She pushed against the bottom of the river with her feet. She lifted herself up to the surface—with the crocodile still hanging onto her arm. She managed to breathe in some fresh air before the croc pulled her down and the death roll began again.

13   Several times the crocodile repeated its death roll. Each time, Rossi waited until the spinning stopped, then pushed up toward the surface. Meanwhile, her friend swam out to help her. Together the two of them wrestled the crocodile back toward shore. At last they managed to drag themselves out of the water. But when Rossi finally wrenched free of the crocodile, she left most of her arm behind. Her friend saw the crocodile open its jaws and swallow the mass of bone, muscle, and skin that it had been grasping between its teeth.

14   Survival stories like Sandy Rossi's and Hilton Graham's are rare. What happened to Ginger Faye Meadows is more typical. Meadows was an American who took a trip to western Australia. While there, she went for a swim along the Kimberly Coast. When she dove into the water, however, a crocodile was waiting for her. Meadows died in the saltie's huge jaws.

15   Clearly, you need to be very careful when you're in crocodile country. It's not enough to avoid the logs in the water. You must also be sure that the logs don't have ears, nostrils, and two yellow eyes.

If you have been timed while reading this article, enter your reading time below. Then turn to the Words-per-Minute Table on page 147 and look up your reading speed (words per minute). Enter your reading speed on the graph on page 148.

Reading Time: Lesson 11

——————— : ———————
Minutes   Seconds

A | Finding the Main Idea

One statement below expresses the main idea of the article. One statement is too general, or too broad. The other statement explains only part of the article; it is too narrow. Label the statements using the following key:

M—Main Idea   **B—Too Broad**   **N—Too Narrow**

_____ 1. Because crocodiles can hold their breath for up to one hour, they can easily drown their victims, including human beings.

_____ 2. Tourists visiting some countries must be given strong warnings about the dangers from crocodiles, especially near rivers.

_____ 3. Crocodiles kill their victims—including people—by grasping them in their jaws and drowning them, and few whom they attack escape.

_____ Score 15 points for a correct M answer.

_____ Score 5 points for each correct B or N answer.

_____ **Total Score:** Finding the Main Idea

B | Recalling Facts

How well do you remember the facts in the article? Put an X in the box next to the answer that correctly completes each statement about the article.

1. Crocodiles are found in
   ☐ a. Asia, Australia, and Africa.
   ☐ b. Australia and South America.
   ☒ c. Africa, Asia, and South America.

2. The largest crocodiles are up to
   ☐ a. 18 feet long and weigh about 2,000 pounds.
   ☐ b. 28 feet long and weigh about 4,000 pounds.
   ☐ c. 28 feet long and weigh about 6,000 pounds.

3. Usually, a crocodile's victim dies from
   ☒ a. drowning.
   ☐ b. loss of blood.
   ☐ c. a heart attack.

4. Peta Lynn Mann saved Hilton Graham from a crocodile when the
   ☐ a. girl struck the crocodile with a paddle.
   ☐ b. man managed to pry the jaws open.
   ☒ c. crocodile loosened its hold for a moment.

5. Sandy Rossi escaped from a crocodile but
   ☐ a. the crocodile bit off her right leg.
   ☒ b. lost her left arm in the process.
   ☐ c. her back was riddled with toothmarks.

Score 5 points for each correct answer.

_____ **Total Score:** Recalling Facts

109

C | Making Inferences

When you combine your own experience with information from a text to draw a conclusion that is not directly stated in that text, you are making an inference. Below are five statements that may or may not be inferences based on information in the article. Label the statements using the following key:

C—Correct Inference   F—Faulty Inference

_____ 1. If you feed a crocodile today, you can be certain that it will not want to eat for six months.

_____ 2. Crocodiles in the wild have never killed anyone in the United States.

_____ 3. Ancient crocodiles may have killed and eaten dinosaurs.

_____ 4. One way to make a crocodile harmless, at least for a time, would be to lock a powerful chain around its jaws, forcing them shut.

_____ 5. You could safely observe crocodiles close up by crawling out on a tree branch hanging two or three feet over the river in which they are swimming.

Score 5 points for each correct answer.

_____ **Total Score:** Making Inferences

D | Using Words Precisely

Each numbered sentence below contains an underlined word or phrase from the article. Following the sentence are three definitions. One definition is closest to the meaning of the underlined word. One definition is opposite or nearly opposite. Label those two definitions using the following key; do not label the remaining definition.

C—Closest   O—Opposite or Nearly Opposite

1. Then, in one <u>explosive</u> burst, it opened its jaws and sank its teeth deep into the woman's flesh.

_____ a. exclusive

_____ b. as if exploding

_____ c. held in

2. Around and around it twirls, down through the water in a <u>corkscrew</u> spin.

_____ a. straight; direct

_____ b. irregular

_____ c. spiral; twisting

3. His arm was crushed. He had <u>internal</u> injuries.

_____ a. on the inside

_____ b. outside

_____ c. serious

4. And his back was <u>riddled</u> with teethmarks the size of golf balls.

_____ a. scraped raw

_____ b. whole; unbroken

_____ c. cut with many small holes made by a sharp object

5. Usually a crocodile is <u>relentless</u> in its attack.

_____ a. fickle; changeable

_____ b. rushed; hurried

_____ c. constant; unchanging

_____ Score 3 points for each correct C answer.

_____ Score 2 points for each correct O answer.

_____ **Total Score:** Using Words Precisely

Enter the four total scores in the spaces below, and add them together to find your Reading Comprehension Score. Then record your score on the graph on page 149.

Score	Question Type	Lesson 11
_____	Finding the Main Idea	
_____	Recalling Facts	
_____	Making Inferences	
_____	Using Words Precisely	
_____	**Reading Comprehension Score**	

Author's Approach

Put an X in the box next to the correct answer.

1. What is the authors' purpose in writing "Crocodiles: The Jaws of Death"?

☐ a. to explain where in the world any crocodiles can be found

☐ b. to persuade readers never to visit Australia

☐ c. to alert readers to the dangerous habits of certain crocodiles

2. In this article, "His back was riddled with teethmarks the size of golf balls" means that

☐ a. how his back came to have teethmarks was a riddle.

☐ b. the teethmarks on his back were as wide as golf balls

☐ c. the teethmarks on his back were perfectly round, like golf balls

3. What do the authors imply by saying "You must also be sure that the logs don't have ears, nostrils, and two yellow eyes"?

☐ a. Logs with ears, nostrils, and two yellow eyes are not really logs; they are crocodiles.

☐ b. It is not always easy to see whether a floating log has ears, nostrils, and eyes, so you must get very close to each one to inspect it.

☐ c. Logs with ears, nostrils, and two blue or brown eyes are not dangerous.

4. Choose the statement below that best describes the authors' position in paragraph 4.

☐ a. People who wander carelessly in crocodile territory deserve to be eaten.

☐ b. As a rule, the most dangerous crocodile is the largest kind, the saltie.

☐ c. Humans must treat all three kinds of killer crocodiles with a great deal of respect and caution.

_____ Number of correct answers

Record your personal assessment of your work on the Critical Thinking Chart on page 150.

Summarizing and Paraphrasing

Put an X in the box next to the correct answer for questions 1 and 3. Follow the directions provided for question 2.

1. Below are summaries of the article. Choose the summary that says all the most important things about the article but in the fewest words.

☐ a. Reports of humans killed by certain kinds of crocodiles should cause people to respect and fear crocodiles.

☐ b. Two kinds of crocodiles that attack humans live in Asia, and a third lives in Africa.

☐ c. Crocodiles killed two swimmers in Australia, but a boater in Australia and a swimmer in Africa managed to escape, although seriously injured.

2. Reread paragraph 7 in the article. Below, write a summary of the paragraph in no more than 25 words.

_____

_____

_____

_____

Reread your summary and decide whether it covers the important ideas in the paragraph. Next, decide how to shorten the summary to 15 words or less without leaving out any essential information. Write this summary below.

_____

_____

_____

3. Choose the sentence that correctly restates the following sentence from the article, describing crocodiles: "Once they select a victim, . . . they are reluctant to let it get away."

☐ a. It is almost impossible to get the crocodile to change its mind and go after another target.

☐ b. A crocodile's victim rarely escapes.

☐ c. When a crocodile gets hungry, it goes after the first victim it can catch.

_____ Number of correct answers

Record your personal assessment of your work on the Critical Thinking Chart on page 150.

Critical Thinking

Put an X in the box next to the correct answer for questions 1 and 2. Follow the directions provided for the other questions.

1. Which of the following statements from the article is an opinion rather than a fact?

☐ a. In 1993 Rossi was serving as tutor and nanny to two American children in Zaire, Africa.

☐ b. Since the late 1970s, these crocodiles have killed and eaten at least eight people.

☐ c. With all those teeth, you might think a crocodile chews its victims to pieces.

2. From the article, you can predict that if a crocodile attacks someone swimming near you,

☐ a. it will attack you next.

☐ b. that person will either die or be seriously injured.

☐ c. that person will escape easily by swimming closer to you and confusing the crocodile.

3. Choose from the letters below to correctly complete the following statement. Write the letters on the lines.

On the positive side, _____, but on the negative side _____.

a. even survivors of crocodile attacks are usually seriously injured

b. a few people have survived attacks by crocodiles

c. crocodiles can hold their breath for up to an hour

4. Which paragraph or paragraphs from the article provide evidence that supports your answer to question 2? _____

5. Reread paragraph 7. Then choose from the letters below to correctly complete the following statement. Write the letters on the lines.

According to paragraph 7, _____ because _____.

a. a crocodile does not use its teeth for chewing

b. a crocodile rolls its victim underwater and holds it there

c. a crocodile's victim dies

_____ Number of correct answers

Record your personal assessment of your work on the Critical Thinking Chart on page 150.

Personal Response

A question I would like answered by the friend who saved Sandy Rossi from a crocodile is _____

_____

_____

Self-Assessment

From reading this article, I have learned these facts:

_____

_____

_____

Killer Bees

Running into killer bees would ruin any outdoor activity. These aggressive bees from Africa don't just attack one at a time. They gang up on their victims, attacking by the thousands.

Christopher Graves didn't have time to run away. One moment he was starting up his lawn mower and the next moment he was completely covered with angry, stinging bees. The attack came on August 23, 1994. Graves was at his grandmother's home in Texas. He had planned to cut the grass for her. But when the 20-year-old Graves started the mower, he upset a swarm of bees in the area.

2   Graves saw the first bee come at him. He felt its sting.

3   "In the next blink of my eye," he said, "I was just covered."

4   Indeed, about 4,000 bees had appeared out of nowhere. They buzzed furiously around Graves. They stung him more than 1,000 times. Each sting carried just a small amount of poison. But all together, the stings threatened his life. By the time firefighters arrived and got him to the hospital, Graves was in serious condition.

5   This was not the first time bees had attacked a human, and it would not be the last. In fact, since 1957, more than 1,000 people have been killed in bee attacks. Countless more have fought off angry bees and survived.

6   One survivor was 51-year-old Leonard Salcido. On August 16, 1997, he was mowing his backyard in New Mexico. Salcido knew there was a beehive in the fence at the edge of the lawn. But he wasn't worried about it. It had been there for a long time. In the winter, he and his family gathered honey from it. The noise of the lawn mower never seemed to bother the bees at all.

7   But on this day, the bees went crazy.

8   "It was like a horror movie," said Salcido's daughter. "My dad was mowing the yard when we looked out and saw him running toward the water hose. I ran out of the house and grabbed the hose and tried to spray him down with water. The bees came for me. They were everywhere. The water was not getting them off my dad." By the time Salcido got away from the bees, he had been stung over 100 times.

9   Stories like Graves's and Salcido's are becoming more and more common. That's because there is a new kind of bee in America. Scientists refer to it as the "Africanized bee." But most people just call it the killer bee.

10   Long ago there were no honeybees of any kind in North or South America. Then, in the 1600s, Europeans brought some over. These European bees quickly adapted to life in North America. They set up colonies. They built hives and produced honey. But down in Latin America, these bees did not do so well. They didn't care for the hot, humid climate. As a result, little honey was produced in Latin America. If folks there wanted honey, they had to ship it in from the north.

11   In the 1950s, scientists hoped to change that situation. They wanted to breed honeybees that liked hot weather. They knew that African bees did well in hot climates. But African bees were much more aggressive than the European variety. They were more

easily disturbed. And when they got angry, they attacked in large numbers.

12 Still, scientists thought the African bees could be helpful. They brought some to a laboratory in Brazil. They never meant to release the bees into the open. Instead, they planned to keep them locked away in the lab. There they could crossbreed them with European bees. In time, they hoped to get a new and improved bee. It would have the gentle personality of European bees. But it would have the African bees' love of hot weather.

13 It sounded like a good plan. But something went wrong. In 1957, a group of African bees escaped from the lab. They flew out into the wild. Soon they began to take over local hives. The result was not what scientists had been hoping for. The new bees certainly liked hot weather. But their personalities were far from mellow. One scientist called them "honeybees with an attitude."

14 "All honeybees have bad days," the scientist explained. But for the new Africanized bees, every day is a bad day. These bees are 10 times as aggressive as European bees. It takes European bees about 19 seconds to get irritated enough to sting. It takes Africanized bees just 3 seconds.

15 And that's not all. European bees will chase a person for only about 400 meters. Africanized bees will follow their targets for a metric mile.

16 Africanized bees work in large groups. So people are rarely stung by just one or two. If these bees feel threatened, they send huge numbers rushing out to attack.

17 Could the news get any worse? Yes. Consider this: it takes just one Africanized bee to drastically change a whole colony of European bees. Experts think that's what happened in Leonard Salcido's case. One killer bee might have found its way into his peaceful backyard hive. In just 45 days, that one bee could have transformed the colony. Instead of European bees, the hive would have been filled with Africanized bees.

18 Experts point out that killer bees attack only when they feel threatened. So the key is to stay far away from them. That advice would have helped Chisha Chang. On August 3, 1998, the 88-year-old Chang found a beehive attached to his barbecue grill. He thought he could remove it himself. So he put a plastic bag over his head for protection. Then he reached down to pull out the hive.

19 Suddenly, dozens and dozens of bees flew out at Chang. They swarmed all over him. Many got up inside the plastic bag. They stung him all over his face and head.

20 Police and firefighters were called to the scene. Said one firefighter, "I would describe him as having a hive of bees on his face. You could not see his eyes or his nose. It was like a hive being taken out of a tree and placed on his head."

21 A rescue worker managed to pull the bag off Chang's face and move him to safety. Luckily, Chang survived the attack. Later, a specially trained beekeeper removed the hive from the grill. He estimated that it contained 70,000 bees.

22 Today, killer bees are a fact of life in Texas, New Mexico, Arizona, and California. But the rest of the United States doesn't have much to worry about. Africanized bees still love hot weather. Whenever they stray to colder regions, they die. And that's good news for anyone who likes to mow the lawn in peace.

If you have been timed while reading this article, enter your reading time below. Then turn to the Words-per-Minute Table on page 147 and look up your reading speed (words per minute). Enter your reading speed on the graph on page 148.

Reading Time: Lesson 12

———— : ————
Minutes   Seconds

A Finding the Main Idea

One statement below expresses the main idea of the article. One statement is too general, or too broad. The other statement explains only part of the article; it is too narrow. Label the statements using the following key:

M—Main Idea   **B—Too Broad**   **N—Too Narrow**

_____ 1. Bees, especially killer bees, have become a serious problem in the United States.

_____ 2. Killer bees, brought to America from Africa, sometimes attack in great numbers. They sting and kill many people in hot parts of the United States.

_____ 3. Killer bees may chase their victims for a metric mile.

_____ Score 15 points for a correct M answer.

_____ Score 5 points for each correct B or N answer.

_____ **Total Score:** Finding the Main Idea

B Recalling Facts

How well do you remember the facts in the article? Put an X in the box next to the answer that correctly completes each statement about the article.

1. Scientists who brought the killer bees to America had hoped to create a new kind of bee that
   - ☐ a. would be more aggressive than the honeybee.
   - ☐ b. did well in hot climates.
   - ☐ c. would be gentler than the honeybee.

2. Scientists sometimes call the killer bee the
   - ☐ a. Africanized bee.
   - ☐ b. honeybee.
   - ☐ c. European bee.

3. A group of killer bees escaped from scientific laboratories in
   - ☐ a. Florida.
   - ☐ b. Brazil.
   - ☐ c. Mexico.

4. One reason why killer bees are more dangerous than honeybees is
   - ☐ a. the amount of poison each bee holds.
   - ☐ b. their inability to live in cold climates.
   - ☐ c. their aggressive attitude.

5. To change a hive of European bees to a killer-bee hive takes
   - ☐ a. just one bee and 45 days.
   - ☐ b. two bees and six months.
   - ☐ c. about 20 bees and about a month.

Score 5 points for each correct answer.

_____ **Total Score:** Recalling Facts

C | Making Inferences

When you combine your own experience with information from a text to draw a conclusion that is not directly stated in that text, you are making an inference. Below are five statements that may or may not be inferences based on information in the article. Label the statements using the following key:

C—Correct Inference   **F—Faulty Inference**

_____ 1. One sure way to save someone from killer bees is to spray the victim with water from a hose.

_____ 2. Most people can easily outrun a swarm of angry killer bees.

_____ 3. Killer bees communicate with one another.

_____ 4. People in the southern states should avoid disturbing any beehives.

_____ 5. Scientists will never able to improve killer bees to make them less aggressive.

Score 5 points for each correct answer.

_____ **Total Score:** Making Inferences

D | Using Words Precisely

Each numbered sentence below contains an underlined word or phrase from the article. Following the sentence are three definitions. One definition is closest to the meaning of the underlined word. One definition is opposite or nearly opposite. Label those two definitions using the following key; do not label the remaining definition.

C—Closest   **O—Opposite or Nearly Opposite**

1. <u>Countless</u> more have fought off angry bees and survived.

_____ a. hardly any; no

_____ b. so many that the number cannot easily be counted

_____ c. a few hundred

2. These European bees quickly <u>adapted to</u> life in North America.

_____ a. became used to

_____ b. discovered

_____ c. fought against

3. They didn't care for the hot, <u>humid</u> climate.

_____ a. dry

_____ b. strange

_____ c. damp or muggy

4. The new bees certainly liked hot weather. But their personalities were far from <u>mellow</u>.

_____ a. easygoing

_____ b. angry and irritable

_____ c. heat loving

5. Later, a specially trained beekeeper removed the hive from the grill. He <u>estimated</u> that it contained 70,000 bees.

_____ a. hoped

_____ b. knew for certain

_____ c. guessed

_____ Score 3 points for each correct C answer.

_____ Score 2 points for each correct O answer.

_____ **Total Score:** Using Words Precisely

Enter the four total scores in the spaces below, and add them together to find your Reading Comprehension Score. Then record your score on the graph on page 149.

Score	Question Type	Lesson 12
_____	Finding the Main Idea	
_____	Recalling Facts	
_____	Making Inferences	
_____	Using Words Precisely	
_____	**Reading Comprehension Score**	

Author's Approach

Put an X in the box next to the correct answer.

1. The authors use the first sentence of the article to
   - ☐ a. inform readers about the danger of killer bees.
   - ☐ b. describe the personality of Christopher Graves.
   - ☐ c. make readers curious about why Graves would run away.

2. What do the authors mean by the statement "Indeed, about 4,000 bees had appeared out of nowhere"?
   - ☐ a. These bees had the power to appear and disappear at will.
   - ☐ b. The bees attacked suddenly and without warning.
   - ☐ c. The victim had been sleeping and hadn't noticed the bees coming closer.

3. Judging by statements from the article "Killer Bees," you can conclude that the authors want the reader to think that
   - ☐ a. the scientists should not have allowed any killer bees to escape.
   - ☐ b. killer bees will eventually be replaced by honeybees.
   - ☐ c. people cannot fight killer bees with any success.

4. The authors tell this story mainly by
   - ☐ a. comparing different topics.
   - ☐ b. using their imagination and creativity.
   - ☐ c. telling different stories about the same topic.

_____ Number of correct answers

Record your personal assessment of your work on the Critical Thinking Chart on page 150.

Summarizing and Paraphrasing

Follow the directions provided for questions 1 and 2. Put an X in the box next to the correct answer for question 3.

1. Complete the following one-sentence summary of the article using the lettered phrases from the phrase bank below. Write the letters on the lines.

> **Phrase Bank**
>
> a. a description of a killer bee attack
> b. how killer bees became a problem in the United States
> c. the fact that killer bees cannot live in cold climates

The article "Killer Bees" begins with _____, goes on to explain _____, and ends with _____.

2. Reread paragraph 17 in the article. Below, write a summary of the paragraph in no more than 25 words.

_____

_____

_____

_____

Reread your summary and decide whether it covers the important ideas in the paragraph. Next, decide how to shorten the summary to 15 words or less without leaving out any essential information. Write this summary below.

_____

_____

_____

3. Choose the best one-sentence paraphrase for the following sentence from the article: "One scientist called [the killer bees] 'honeybees with an attitude.' "

☐ a. One scientist says that killer bees are much like honeybees, only they are bad tempered.

☐ b. Most scientists think that killer bees are just like honeybees.

☐ c. Scientists say that one way killer bees are similar to honeybees is their attitude.

_____ Number of correct answers

Record your personal assessment of your work on the Critical Thinking Chart on page 150.

Critical Thinking

Follow the directions provided for questions 1, 3, and 5. Put an X in the box next to the correct answer for the other questions.

1. For each statement below, write O if it expresses an opinion or write F if it expresses a fact.

_____ a. There is nothing more painful and frightening than to be stung by thousands of bees.

_____ b. The scientists who brought the killer bees to America should be ashamed of themselves.

_____ c. When killer bees get angry, thousands of them attack at once.

2. From the information in paragraph 22, you can predict that

☐ a. people in the northern states will someday face the problem of killer bees.

☐ b. killer bees will die out in the southern states.

☐ c. killer bees will never be a big problem in northern states.

3. Choose from the letters below to correctly complete the following statement. Write the letters on the lines.

In the article, _____ and _____ are different.

a. European bees

b. Africanized bees

c. honeybees

4. What was the cause of the many bee stings on Chisha Chang's head?

☐ a. The bees had become trapped under the plastic bag over his head.

☐ b. Killer bees always attack only the victim's head.

☐ c. Chang had hit the bees' hive with his head.

5. Which paragraphs from the article provide evidence that supports your answer to question 4? _____

_____ Number of correct answers

Record your personal assessment of your work on the Critical Thinking Chart on page 150.

Personal Response

I know the feeling that Christopher Graves had when the killer bees attacked him because _____

_____

_____

_____

Self-Assessment

One good question about this article that was not asked would be

_____

_____

_____

and the answer is _____

_____

_____

_____

CRITICAL THINKING

Cougars on the Prowl

Cougars were once quite common throughout the United States and southern Canada. As settlers moved in and populated these areas the cougars' numbers dropped. Today, cougars are found mainly in western U.S. states and Canadian provinces.

Iris Kenna liked to watch rare birds. To find them, the 56-year-old school counselor often hiked in the Cuyamaca Rancho State Park near San Diego. But in 1995 Kenna found something she wasn't looking for—a cougar. Caught by surprise, Kenna never had a chance. The wild cat dragged her off the path and into some dense brush. With its sharp claws and piercing teeth, the cougar soon claimed Kenna's life. At some point in the struggle, it ripped off part of her scalp. Park rangers later found Kenna's dead body covered with bite marks.

2   Laura Smalls was only five years old when she was attacked by a cougar. In 1986 she went exploring with her parents in California's Caspers Wilderness Park. For a few seconds, she wandered off by herself. That was a mistake. A cougar leapt at her and pulled her into the bushes. "All I heard was a rustle in the bushes behind me," Laura recalled. "A split second later [the cougar] had me by the head."

3   Luckily, Laura's screams brought her parents running. They managed to beat off the cougar with a stick. That probably saved the girl's life. Still, the attack left her blind in her right eye. It also left her partially paralyzed.

4   Cougars go by many names. They are called mountain lions, catamounts, panthers, and pumas. Whatever name you prefer, keep in mind that these are dangerous creatures. They are fierce meat eaters. They hunt deer, elk, rabbits, and other animals. Cougars are patient in their quest for food. A cougar will stalk its prey until just the right moment. Then it will lunge at the victim's throat or neck. Given a choice, a cougar will choose the weakest prey and attack from behind.

5   Cougars don't often attack human beings. But when they do, they usually go for women or children. Men, who tend to be bigger and taller, may simply look too tough for a cougar to take on.

6   Cougar attacks have increased in recent years. This is especially true in western states. Each year, more people move there. New homes are being built closer and closer to where cougars live. So bloody encounters are likely to become more frequent.

7   What would happen if you found yourself eyeball-to-eyeball with a cougar? Would you have any chance of surviving the attack? Actually, you'd have a good chance—if you knew what to do. The first rule is never run away. That's what a cougar's other victims do. You don't want to act like a deer or a rabbit. If you do, the cougar will quickly run you down and finish you off.

8   Your best strategy is to look as big as possible. Stand tall, with your arms raised. Then slowly back away. If the cougar still attacks, stay on your feet and fight back! A cougar is used to attacking helpless prey. It may become confused, even frightened, if you put up a fight. Poke it in the eyes, kick it in the groin, punch it in the mouth. Pick up a heavy stick and imagine you are taking batting practice—with the cougar's head as the baseball. Most cougars will flee when faced with stiff resistance.

9   For a dramatic example, take the case of Larrane Leech. She ran a day-care center

out of her home in British Columbia. Leech loved the outdoors. She wanted the children to enjoy it, too. And they did. Their favorite activity was circle time. The kids would sit outdoors in a circle and pass around an eagle feather. Whoever held it could talk about anything he or she wanted.

10 On July 3, 1991, Leech took five children for a walk to the Fraser River. Her German shepherd puppy, Pal, went with them. The children picked berries along the way. Finally, Leech called to them to "get in our circle." One little girl, however, ran off toward some trees. Leech hurried to retrieve her.

11 As Leech headed back to the circle with the girl, her face froze in terror. A young cougar had appeared from the bushes. It had a two-year-old boy named Mikey pinned to the ground. From where Leech stood, she couldn't see Mikey's face. She couldn't tell if he was alive or dead. None of the other children seemed to understand what was happening. To them, the cougar looked like an overgrown house cat. "Stop licking Mikey's face," one of them giggled.

12 Leech didn't stop to think about her own safety. Her only thought was to rescue Mikey. She charged toward the cougar, intending to grab its tail. At the last second, though, she grabbed it by the scruff of its neck. She shook the cougar from side to side. "I couldn't tell if he had Mikey's face in his mouth, or if he would rip him apart," she later recalled. "So I just shook him."

13 As it turned out, the cougar had not yet bitten Mikey. It was a young cougar; it had not learned to make a fast, efficient attack. Instead, it was licking the boy's face clean in preparation for its first bite. When Leech grabbed its neck, it shifted into a more vicious attack mode. It whirled toward her, hissing and spitting. As it spun, its claws caught Mikey in the face. These claws also nicked Lisa, not quite two years old, under her eye. Leech fell backward as the cougar's powerful paw smacked her across her right ear.

14 The children now realized that this was no game. They began screaming in terror. They raced to hide behind Leech. "Stay behind me!" she shouted to them. "Don't move."

15 Leech managed to grab the cougar's front paws. She straightened out her arms, holding the animal as far away from her body as she could. The cougar growled angrily and tried to pull free from her grip. Her arms and legs ached as the cat thrashed furiously back and forth. Yet Leech held on, knowing that if the cougar broke away from her it could kill the children. "Leave us alone," she screamed at the cat, "and we'll leave you alone!"

16 Calling on all her remaining strength, Leech shoved the cougar at her German shepherd. "Pal, do something!" she cried. As Pal began to bark, the cougar scrambled to its feet. Then it dashed away, with Pal still barking after it.

17 Larrane Leech had done the right thing. By putting up a fight and yelling in a loud voice, she had scared the cougar. Amazingly, she suffered only minor cuts and scratches. Mikey needed 40 stitches. Little Lisa needed 20. All the children were very fortunate. If Leech had not acted as she did, the incident could have ended in tragedy.

18 The Canadian government knows a hero when it sees one. It awarded Larrane Leech its Star of Courage for "outstanding bravery." Leech modestly noted that "any parent would have done the same." Perhaps. But how many parents have ever gone face-to-fang with a wild cougar?

If you have been timed while reading this article, enter your reading time below. Then turn to the Words-per-Minute Table on page 147 and look up your reading speed (words per minute). Enter your reading speed on the graph on page 148.

Reading Time: Lesson 13

——— : ———
Minutes   *Seconds*

A Finding the Main Idea

One statement below expresses the main idea of the article. One statement is too general, or too broad. The other statement explains only part of the article; it is too narrow. Label the statements using the following key:

M—Main Idea   **B—Too Broad**   **N—Too Narrow**

_____ 1. Cougars, sometimes called mountain lions, have become an increasing problem in western states.

_____ 2. Because cougars sometimes attack human beings, hikers in western states should stay alert and ready.

_____ 3. When cougars attack human beings, they usually attack women or children, possibly because these targets tend to be smaller than men.

_____ Score 15 points for a correct M answer.

_____ Score 5 points for each correct B or N answer.

_____ **Total Score:** Finding the Main Idea

B Recalling Facts

How well do you remember the facts in the article? Put an X in the box next to the answer that correctly completes each statement about the article.

1. Another name for a cougar is a
   ☐ a. coyote.
   ☐ b. marmoset.
   ☐ c. puma.

2. Cougar attacks have become more frequent because
   ☐ a. people have moved closer to cougars.
   ☐ b. cougars are becoming more violent.
   ☐ c. Western weather has changed.

3. If you are confronted by a cougar,
   ☐ a. run away as fast as possible.
   ☐ b. shoot it immediately.
   ☐ c. raise your arms and back away.

4. Larrane Leech ran a daycare center in
   ☐ a. Oregon.
   ☐ b. British Columbia.
   ☐ c. Arizona.

5. Larrane Leech was awarded the
   ☐ a. Star of Courage.
   ☐ b. Presidential Medal.
   ☐ c. Congressional Medal of Honor.

Score 5 points for each correct answer.

_____ **Total Score:** Recalling Facts

C | Making Inferences

When you combine your own experience with information from a text to draw a conclusion that is not directly stated in that text, you are making an inference. Below are five statements that may or may not be inferences based on information in the article. Label the statements using the following key:

C—Correct Inference   F—Faulty Inference

_____ 1. Cougars used to be gentle, harmless animals before people moved into their territory.

_____ 2. Cougars always kill their prey; they never leave a victim alive.

_____ 3. The conflict between cougars and people will most likely increase in the coming years.

_____ 4. Cougars enjoy the challenge of a good fight with a victim.

_____ 5. Puppies sometimes need to be taught to protect their owners and friends from danger.

Score 5 points for each correct answer.

_____ **Total Score:** Making Inferences

D | Using Words Precisely

Each numbered sentence below contains an underlined word or phrase from the article. Following the sentence are three definitions. One definition is closest to the meaning of the underlined word. One definition is opposite or nearly opposite. Label those two definitions using the following key; do not label the remaining definition.

C—Closest   O—Opposite or Nearly Opposite

1. The wild cat dragged her off the path and into some <u>dense</u> brush.

_____ a. thin; sparse

_____ b. thick; heavy

_____ c. scratchy

2. It also left her partially <u>paralyzed</u>.

_____ a. afraid

_____ b. able to move freely

_____ c. unable to move

3. It also left her <u>partially</u> paralyzed.

_____ a. sadly

_____ b. partly

_____ c. entirely

4. Her arms and legs ached as the cat <u>thrashed</u> furiously back and forth.

_____ a. swayed gently

_____ b. played

_____ c. moved violently

5. For a <u>dramatic</u> example, take the case of Larrane Leech.

_____ a. dull

_____ b. striking; exciting

_____ c. confusing

_____ Score 3 points for each correct C answer.

_____ Score 2 points for each correct O answer.

_____ **Total Score:** Using Words Precisely

Enter the four total scores in the spaces below, and add them together to find your Reading Comprehension Score. Then record your score on the graph on page 149.

Score	Question Type	Lesson 13
_____	Finding the Main Idea	
_____	Recalling Facts	
_____	Making Inferences	
_____	Using Words Precisely	
_____	**Reading Comprehension Score**	

Author's Approach

Put an X in the box next to the correct answer.

1. The main purpose of the first paragraph is to
    ☐ a.   warn readers never to hike in California.
    ☐ b.   describe the typical day's work for park rangers.
    ☐ c.   persuade readers of the dangers of cougars.

2. From the statements below, choose the one that you believe the authors would agree with.
    ☐ a.   Cougars are not very brave.
    ☐ b.   Children often do not recognize dangers in the wild.
    ☐ c.   Cougars rarely attack unless someone disturbs them.

3. Choose the statement below that is the weakest argument for fighting back if a cougar attacks you.
    ☐ a.   Cougars can be scared away by a strong defense.
    ☐ b.   Newspaper reporters may report what happened.
    ☐ c.   Other people have saved themselves and others by fighting back.

4. The authors tell this story mainly by
    ☐ a.   comparing different topics.
    ☐ b.   using their imagination and creativity.
    ☐ c.   giving different examples about the topic.

_____ Number of correct answers

Record your personal assessment of your work on the Critical Thinking Chart on page 150.

Summarizing and Paraphrasing

Follow the directions provided for question 1. Put an X in the box next to the correct answer for the other questions.

1. Complete the following one-sentence summary of the article using the lettered phrases from the phrase bank below. Write the letters on the lines.

> **Phrase Bank**
> a. accounts of vicious cougar attacks
> b. a report of a successful defense
> c. the best defense against an attack by a cougar

The article "Cougars on the Prowl" begins with _____, goes on to explain _____, and ends with _____.

2. Read the statement from the article below. Then read the paraphrase of that statement. Choose the reason that best tells why the paraphrase does not say the same thing as the statement.

Statement: The best way to survive a cougar attack is to stand up tall and fight back.

Paraphrase: It's possible to survive a cougar attack.

☐ a. Paraphrase says too much.

☐ b. Paraphrase doesn't say enough.

☐ c. Paraphrase doesn't agree with the statement.

3. Choose the best one-sentence paraphrase for the following sentence from the article: "Men, who tend to be bigger and taller, may simply look too tough for a cougar to take on."

☐ a. Cougars tend not to attack men because their flesh is too tough.

☐ b. Cougars may be afraid to attack men, who are usually bigger and taller.

☐ c. If a big, tall, tough man looks at a cougar, the cougar will take off.

> _____ Number of correct answers
>
> Record your personal assessment of your work on the Critical Thinking Chart on page 150.

Critical Thinking

Put an X in the box next to the correct answer for questions 1, 3, and 4. Follow the directions provided for question 2.

1. How is "Cougars on the Prowl" related to the theme of this book?

☐ a. Cougar attacks have left many victims dead or badly injured.

☐ b. Many cougars live in the western states.

☐ c. The Canadian government gave Larrane Leech an award.

2. Think about cause-effect relationships in the article. Fill in the blanks in the cause-effect chart, drawing from the letters below.

Cause	Effect
A cougar attacked five-year-old Laura Smalls, grabbing her by her head.	_____
_____ Larraine Leech fought off a cougar, saving several children	We can expect more frequent meetings of cougars and humans. _____

a. She was awarded Canada's Star of Courage.

b. More new homes are being built closer to where cougars live.

c. The attack left her blind in one eye and partially paralyzed.

3. If you were a hiker in a forest in the West, how could you use the information in the article to choose your companions?

☐ a. Like Larrane Leech, take several preschoolers with you.

☐ b. Like Laura Smalls, take your parents with you.

☐ c. Like Larrane Leech, take a dog with you.

4. What did you have to do to answer question 2?

☐ a. find an opinion (what someone thinks about something)

☐ b. find a description (how something looks)

☐ c. find causes and effects (what happened and why)

_____ Number of correct answers

Record your personal assessment of your work on the Critical Thinking Chart on page 150.

Personal Response

How do you think the girl who ran from Leech's group felt when she realized that deadly cougars were in the forest?

_____

_____

_____

Self-Assessment

When reading the article, I was having trouble with _____

_____

_____

_____

Scorpions: Killers in the Desert

Ross Brown ran up to his mother, holding his finger and crying. At first, Karen Brown guessed that he had been bitten or stung by some sort of insect. But when she looked closely, she couldn't see any mark on the boy's finger. Karen figured Ross, who was only one week shy of his first birthday, was simply overtired. But soon the boy's crying turned to screaming. He began to vomit and shake violently all over. That was when Karen knew something was seriously wrong with her son.

2   It was May 1994. Karen and her husband, Don, had been packing the

This scorpion mom carries her newborn brood on her back. These babies are lucky. Because their mother is in an exhibit and will be fed, they don't have to worry about her forgetting family ties and eating them.

family car when Ross began crying. The Browns were about to head home after a trip to Mexico. They had loved their weekend stay in the desert along the Gulf of California. But suddenly they were in a life-or-death race to save their son.

3   At first, the Browns looked for a local hospital. When they could not find one, they decided to head back to Arizona. As the Browns sped north to the border, Ross grew steadily worse. His eyes rolled back and forth in his head. His nose and mouth foamed. He had trouble breathing. His skin turned pale, and his heart raced furiously.

4   The Browns had no way of knowing it at the time, but Ross had been stung by a scorpion. Long ago, the Maya people, who lived in an area located in what today is Mexico and Central America, had a word for the scorpion. It meant "sign of the death god." There are about 1,500 types of scorpions in the world. They all have poisonous venom. But only about 25 kinds have venom strong enough to kill a human being. Most of these scorpions are found in India, Brazil, and North Africa. In such places,

thousands of people die each year from scorpion stings.

5   One of the lethal scorpions is also found in the deserts of Mexico and Arizona. It is the bark scorpion. It got this name because it often lives under the loose bark of dead trees. The sting of a bark scorpion leaves no visible mark on its victim.

6   All scorpions are night creatures. They wait until dark to come out of hiding and eat. Sometimes they fight each other, with the winner eating the loser. Other times they use their venomous tails to kill beetles, wasps, spiders, and crickets.

7   Scorpions do not wander far away to hunt. Often they travel only a few feet from their home. They identify a spot they like and then settle down for the night, waiting for something to kill. If nothing comes along before sunrise, they'll go home. Scorpions see poorly, but they are good hunters nonetheless. They use their body hair to detect changes in the movement of the air. That's how they sense the presence of prey. If something does come along, the scorpion will seize it with its two pincers.

8   All scorpions are mean. They don't like anyone—not even each other. If hungry, a mother scorpion will eat her own children. After mating, the female will sometimes eat the male. Small scorpions learn to stay out of the way of larger ones.

9   Scorpions have been crawling the earth for 450 million years. That means they were here long before dinosaurs. It's easy to see how scorpions have survived so long. They really are amazing creatures. For one thing, scorpions are almost impossible to kill. You can't drown them. They can live underwater for two days. And they can survive both extreme cold and heat. In one test, a scorpion was left frozen in a block of ice for three weeks. When the ice was melted with a blowtorch, the scorpion simply picked itself up and crawled away. Scorpions have been found on mountains as high as 16,000 feet. They have also been found in cracks in the earth as deep as 2,500 feet. Scorpions are independent too. They can store enough energy to go without eating for more than a year. And they can survive almost forever without drinking water.

10   Scorpions, which are about two to five inches long, don't go looking for trouble with people. But these grumpy little bugs wear a don't-mess-with-me label. At the slightest sign of danger, they will raise their tails with their sharp stingers. They won't hesitate to strike any human being who disturbs them.

11   People can easily stumble into the path of a scorpion. Many scorpions hide out near human activity. They lurk in spots such as carports and woodpiles. They will crawl into sleeping bags or shoes left outdoors. That is why, if you ever camp where scorpions dwell, you should always shake out your shoes before putting them on. Otherwise, you might find a nasty surprise waiting for you. People do get stung by scorpions all the time. For most healthy adults, the sting of a bark scorpion is just a painful nuisance. That same sting, however, can be deadly to an old person or a small child.

12   No one knows what little Ross Brown did. But he must have disturbed a scorpion in some way. In any case, a bark scorpion had stung him. On that long drive back from Mexico, his life was draining away. Don Brown, driving as fast as he dared, at last reached the Arizona border. Karen yelled out to the customs officials for help. Within 40 minutes, Ross was being rushed by ambulance to a nearby clinic. From there he was flown by helicopter to a hospital.

13   By the time Ross arrived at the hospital, it had been five hours since the scorpion had stung him. The doctors took one look at Ross, who was shaking and foaming at the mouth, and knew immediately what had happened. The little boy had all the classic signs of a bark scorpion sting. A doctor gave Ross a shot to neutralize the scorpion's poison. It worked. In just 20 minutes, the boy's jerking stopped and color returned to his face. Worn out, Ross fell asleep. Three hours later, the doctor sent him home with the happy news that he was going to be fine.

14   Still, it had been a close call. As the case of Ross Brown shows, the threat of scorpions should not be taken lightly. Some scorpions can kill.

If you have been timed while reading this article, enter your reading time below. Then turn to the Words-per-Minute Table on page 147 and look up your reading speed (words per minute). Enter your reading speed on the graph on page 148.

Reading Time: Lesson 14

_____ : _____

Minutes   *Seconds*

A Finding the Main Idea

One statement below expresses the main idea of the article. One statement is too general, or too broad. The other statement explains only part of the article; it is too narrow. Label the statements using the following key:

M—Main Idea   **B—Too Broad**   **N—Too Narrow**

_____ 1. With their powerful stingers, scorpions are dangerous and sturdy survivors.

_____ 2. Some creatures are able to survive in the harsh climate of the desert.

_____ 3. Scorpions can live on high mountains as well as deep within the earth.

_____ Score 15 points for a correct M answer.

_____ Score 5 points for each correct B or N answer.

_____ **Total Score:** Finding the Main Idea

B Recalling Facts

How well do you remember the facts in the article? Put an X in the box next to the answer that correctly completes each statement about the article.

1. All scorpions
   - ☐ a. have poisonous venom.
   - ☐ b. live in Brazil and Arizona.
   - ☐ c. have excellent eyesight.

2. Scorpions sense their prey by
   - ☐ a. hearing their victims approach.
   - ☐ b. seeing their victims.
   - ☐ c. feeling air movement on their hairs.

3. If she is hungry, a mother scorpion will
   - ☐ a. eat her children's food herself.
   - ☐ b. eat her own children.
   - ☐ c. leave her children on their own.

4. Scorpions have lived on the earth for about
   - ☐ a. 450 million years.
   - ☐ b. one million years.
   - ☐ c. 45 million years.

5. The bark scorpion
   - ☐ a. looks like a piece of tree bark.
   - ☐ b. can make a sound like a dog's bark.
   - ☐ c. lives under loose bark of dead trees.

Score 5 points for each correct answer.

_____ **Total Score:** Recalling Facts

C Making Inferences

When you combine your own experience with information from a text to draw a conclusion that is not directly stated in that text, you are making an inference. Below are five statements that may or may not be inferences based on information in the article. Label the statements using the following key:

C—Correct Inference   **F—Faulty Inference**

_____ 1. Someone who has trouble breathing and is pale has most likely been stung by a scorpion.

_____ 2. Long ago, the Maya people were afraid of the scorpion, just as people are today.

_____ 3. Since scorpions are night hunters, you need not fear them during the day.

_____ 4. Scorpions are able to adapt to many different climates.

_____ 5. Small dinosaurs may have been victims of scorpion stings.

Score 5 points for each correct answer.

_____ **Total Score:** Making Inferences

D Using Words Precisely

Each numbered sentence below contains an underlined word or phrase from the article. Following the sentence are three definitions. One definition is closest to the meaning of the underlined word. One definition is opposite or nearly opposite. Label those two definitions using the following key; do not label the remaining definition.

C—Closest   **O—Opposite or Nearly Opposite**

1. One of the <u>lethal</u> scorpions is also found in the deserts of Mexico and Arizona.

_____ a. harmless

_____ b. ugly

_____ c. deadly

2. The sting of the bark scorpion leaves no <u>visible</u> mark on its victim.

_____ a. dangerous

_____ b. able to be seen

_____ c. unclear; hidden

3. That's how they sense the <u>presence</u> of prey.

_____ a. nearness

_____ b. absence

_____ c. odor

4. Scorpions are <u>independent</u> too.

_____ a. needful of help

_____ b. playful

_____ c. able to manage without help

5. But these <u>grumpy</u> little bugs wear a don't-mess-with-me label.

_____ a. happy

_____ b. bad-tempered

_____ c. fast

_____ Score 3 points for each correct C answer.

_____ Score 2 points for each correct O answer.

_____ **Total Score:** Using Words Precisely

Enter the four total scores in the spaces below, and add them together to find your Reading Comprehension Score. Then record your score on the graph on page 149.

Score	Question Type	Lesson 14
_____	Finding the Main Idea	
_____	Recalling Facts	
_____	Making Inferences	
_____	Using Words Precisely	
_____	**Reading Comprehension Score**	

Author's Approach

Put an X in the box next to the correct answer.

1. The authors use the first sentence of the article to

☐ a. inform the reader about scorpions.

☐ b. make the reader curious about why Ross was crying.

☐ c. compare two characters, Ross Brown and his mother.

2. Which of the following statements from the article best describes the scorpion's special way of finding a victim?

☐ a. All scorpions are night creatures.

☐ b. If nothing comes along before sunrise, they'll go home.

☐ c. They use their body hair to detect changes in the movement of the air.

3. Judging by statements from the article "Scorpions: Killers in the Desert," you can conclude that the authors want the reader to think that

☐ a. people should never go outdoors where scorpions have been seen.

☐ b. scorpions can be trained to be good pets.

☐ c. people should be careful when enjoying outdoor activities where scorpions may be found.

4. The authors probably wrote this article to

☐ a. warn readers about the dangers of scorpions.

☐ b. explain why the Browns were speeding while returning from their vacation.

☐ c. persuade readers that scorpions are amazing creatures.

_____ Number of correct answers

Record your personal assessment of your work on the Critical Thinking Chart on page 150.

Summarizing and Paraphrasing

Follow the directions provided for question 1. Put an X in the box next to the correct answer for the other questions.

1. Look for the important ideas and events in paragraphs 6 and 7. Summarize those paragraphs in one or two sentences.

_____

_____

_____

_____

2. Below are summaries of the article. Choose the summary that says all the most important things about the article but in the fewest words.

☐ a. Scorpions are amazingly hardy creatures, and some of them, as shown by little Ross Brown's brush with death, are poisonous to humans.

☐ b. Little Ross Brown would have died if his parents hadn't hurried him to a hospital after he was stung by a scorpion during a desert vacation.

☐ c. Scorpions are amazing but deadly creatures.

3. Choose the best one-sentence paraphrase for the following sentence from the article: "Scorpions have been crawling the earth for 450 million years."

☐ a. Some scorpions are more than 450 million years old.

☐ b. 450 million scorpions are crawling the earth.

☐ c. The creatures we call scorpions have been in existence for 450 million years.

_____ Number of correct answers

Record your personal assessment of your work on the Critical Thinking Chart on page 150.

Critical Thinking

Follow the directions provided for questions 1 and 5. Put an X in the box next to the correct answer for the other questions.

1. For each statement below, write O if it expresses an opinion or write F if it expresses a fact.

_____ a. Scorpions survive experiences that would kill humans, such as extreme heat, extreme cold, being underwater for many hours, and doing without food for months.

_____ b. Scorpions are among the most frightening creatures on Earth.

_____ c. Humans would be better off if all scorpions everywhere were killed off.

2. Considering the actions of the customs officials as told in this article, you can predict that

☐ a. other citizens returning across the border will be delayed for hours, even in an emergency.

☐ b. other citizens returning across the border in an emergency will be given prompt attention and help.

☐ c. the government will see there is no need for customs officials and remove them from the border.

3. What is the usual effect of a scorpion's sting on a healthy adult?

☐ a. The victim will die within hours.

☐ b. The victim will slowly lose the ability to resist disease and die within months.

☐ c. The victim will consider the sting merely a painful nuisance.

4. Of the following theme categories, which would this story fit into?

☐ a. Animals are our friends.

☐ b. You can learn a great deal from travel.

☐ c. Never underestimate the danger of a small creature.

5. In which paragraph did you find your information or details to answer question 3? _____

_____ Number of correct answers

Record your personal assessment of your work on the Critical Thinking Chart on page 150.

Personal Response

I can't believe this about scorpions:

_____

_____

_____

_____

Self-Assessment

I'm proud of my answer to question _____ in the _____

section because _____

_____

_____

_____

The Mystery of the Giant Squid

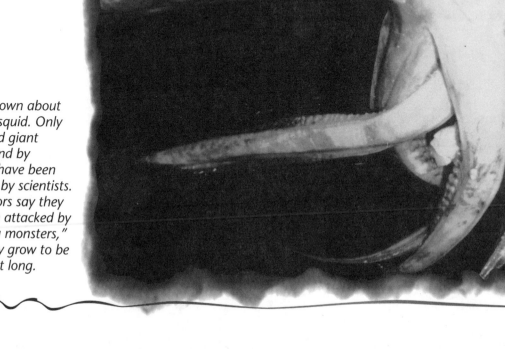

Little is known about the giant squid. Only a few dead giant squid, found by accident, have been examined by scientists. Some sailors say they have been attacked by these "sea monsters," which may grow to be 55–75 feet long.

You don't have to see a giant squid to be afraid of it. All you have to do is read some of the things that have been written about it. Writers have called it a "ghastly looking creature." They have labeled it a "sea monster," a "devilfish," a "horrible beast."

2   In his story "The Sea Raiders," H. G. Wells said the squid's "shape somewhat resembl[es] an octopus," with "very long and flexible tentacles." Jules Verne described it further in his book *Twenty Thousand Leagues Under the Sea*. Verne said its "dreadful arms" are "twice as long as its body." They wriggle like a "nest of serpents." Verne also noted the giant squid's "enormous staring green eyes." Its mouth, he said, is like a huge pair of scissors. And its tongue is lined "with several rows of pointed teeth."

3   In *Denizens of the Deep*, Frank Pullen said the giant creature "does not pursue his prey." Instead, "he waits like some . . . spider in the center of his web of far reaching tentacles." In the novel *Beast*, Peter Benchley described a giant squid "hover[ing] in the ink dark water, waiting." In Benchley's words, "It exist[s] to survive. And to kill."

4   If these descriptions don't frighten you, nothing will! But these accounts come from fiction writers. How much of what they have written is accurate? That's not an easy question to answer. The truth is that we know very little about the giant squid. It is one of the rarest creatures on earth. It lives somewhere in the depths of the ocean, but nobody knows exactly where. Nobody has ever seen one in its natural setting. We know giant squids are down there, however, because every now and then one will come to the surface. It may get caught in a fishing net, or its body may wash up on shore.

5   Clyde F. E. Roper has spent more than 35 years studying giant squids. In 1995 he set up an exhibit for the Smithsonian Institution. He says, "We probably know more about the dinosaurs than about the giant squid." What little we do know, though, is fascinating.

6   To start with, giant squids really are giant. In 1873 one got caught in a fishing net in Newfoundland. It took four men to haul it up out of the water. The squid's body measured eight feet long. Its squirming tentacles added another 24 feet to its length. Two years earlier, an even bigger squid had washed ashore in Newfoundland. Its total length was 52 feet. The all-time record goes to a squid in New Zealand. It measured 55 feet.

7   Even that may not be the outer limit. Fishermen have described giant squids as "much larger than the largest whale, even exceeding in size the hull of a large vessel." Roper thinks some may reach 75 feet. And a professor in Canada has declared that they could grow up to 150 feet!

8   Its length is not all that's big about a giant squid. The creature can weigh up to a ton. Its tentacles are as thick as small tree trunks. And its eyes are the largest of any animal in the world. These eyes are bigger than dinner plates, bigger even than car hubcaps.

9   Giant squids have other interesting features. They can squirt black ink into the water to confuse enemies. If a tentacle

is ripped off, they can grow a new one. Their bodies contain three hearts. Their brains are quite highly developed. And researchers now think they communicate with each other by quickly changing the color of their skin. At times they appear light-colored. But in a flash, they can turn red, brown, or deep purple.

10   There is no question that a giant squid is an awesome creature. But that does not necessarily mean it is dangerous to human beings. In fact, some researchers believe the giant squid is quite shy. One British scientist has called it "a sluggish animal." He believes it stays near the ocean floor. It survives, he thinks, by eating the bodies of small creatures that have died and sunk to the bottom.

11   Other researchers doubt that the giant squid leads such a meek life. If it did, why would it have developed such strength? And so many powerful weapons? After all, its long arms are perfect for wrapping around a victim. These arms are filled with muscles. They could easily put the squeeze on a fairly large animal. The arms are also covered with little suction cups that could help the squid hold onto its prey. The giant squid's mouth is large and shaped like a bird's beak. Out of this mouth comes a tongue covered with so many jagged teeth that anything it touches would be ripped to shreds. (That is one reason why the creature's diet remains a mystery. Scientists have looked inside dead squids' stomachs but have found nothing. Whatever passes through a giant squid's mouth is rapidly reduced to mush.)

12   Over the years, there have been stories of giant squids attacking people. It is not clear if these stories are true. But they are enough to send shivers down your spine. There is, for instance, the story of the *Brunswick*. This ship was making its way across the Pacific Ocean in the early 1930s. One day, the crew spotted a huge squid in the water. It was swimming below the surface, next to the vessel. The giant squid was able to keep up with the *Brunswick*, which was traveling at close to 25 knots, or 30 miles per hour. Suddenly, the squid turned toward the ship. It whipped itself against the hull. Its tentacles tried to grab hold of the metal. The tentacles slipped, however, and the giant squid skidded forward into the propeller. There it was chopped into small pieces.

13   Another attack was reported some years earlier in Newfoundland. A group of fishermen noticed a big object in the water. They thought it might be part of a wrecked ship, so they rowed their small boat over to it. Instantly, the object came to life. It rammed the boat with its beak-like mouth. At the same time, it swung a mighty arm up, encircling the boat. Before the giant squid could drag the boat under, one man managed to cut off the arm. The creature then slipped back down into the water. The fishermen were left holding a writhing 19-foot tentacle.

14   In another report made during World War II, 12 men spent a night floating in the middle of the Atlantic Ocean. The enemy had just sunk their ship. For hours they clung to the edges of a tiny raft. Suddenly, in the dead of night, a giant tentacle emerged from the water. It grabbed one man and pulled him down, never to be seen again.

15   Whether or not these attacks really happened, the giant squid remains an object of fear and awe. As we learn more about the creature, we may find that there is no need for fear. Then we can remove it from the list of "Angry Animals." Or we may discover that all the horror stories are true. In that case, perhaps we should move the giant squid to the top of the list!

If you have been timed while reading this article, enter your reading time below. Then turn to the Words-per-Minute Table on page 147 and look up your reading speed (words per minute). Enter your reading speed on the graph on page 148.

Reading Time: Lesson 15

_____ : _____
Minutes   Seconds

A Finding the Main Idea

One statement below expresses the main idea of the article. One statement is too general, or too broad. The other statement explains only part of the article; it is too narrow. Label the statements using the following key:

M—Main Idea   **B—Too Broad**   **N—Too Narrow**

_____ 1. The little we know about the giant squid, especially its great size, makes us admire and often fear it.

 _____ 2. The giant squid is a sea animal about which we know very little.

_____ 3. Many fiction writers have described the giant squid, but they may have made up many of their details.

_____ Score 15 points for a correct M answer.

_____ Score 5 points for each correct B or N answer.

_____ **Total Score:** Finding the Main Idea

B Recalling Facts

How well do you remember the facts in the article? Put an X in the box next to the answer that correctly completes each statement about the article.

1. Jules Verne compared a squid's tentacles to
☐ a. "many long ropes."
☐ b. a "huge pair of scissors."
☐ c. a "nest of serpents."

2. Squids cannot be seen much because
☐ a. they live in the ocean's depths.
☐ b. they squirt ink at people.
☐ c. their eyes are bigger than dinner plates.

3. Usually, scientists learn about squids by
☐ a. observing them in zoos.
☐ b. observing them in their ocean habitat.
☐ c. examining their dead bodies.

4. The longest squid found to date was
☐ a. 32 feet long.
☐ b. 55 feet long.
☐ c. 150 feet long.

5. Some scientists believe that squids communicate
☐ a. by changing their color.
☐ b. by producing strange "songs" that can be heard miles away under the water.
☐ c. by pounding the water with their arms.

Score 5 points for each correct answer.

_____ **Total Score:** Recalling Facts

C Making Inferences

When you combine your own experience with information from a text to draw a conclusion that is not directly stated in that text, you are making an inference. Below are five statements that may or may not be inferences based on information in the article. Label the statements using the following key:

C—Correct Inference   **F—Faulty Inference**

_____ 1. Novelists who describe giant squids stick faithfully to the truth.

_____ 2. Any aquarium would be delighted to exhibit a giant squid, but this is not yet possible.

_____ 3. Giant squids rarely enter cold waters.

_____ 4. All scientists are confident that reports of giant squids attacking people and ships will be supported by further research.

_____ 5. Increasing pollution of the seas may reduce the number of giant squids.

Score 5 points for each correct answer.

_____ **Total Score:** Making Inferences

D Using Words Precisely

Each numbered sentence below contains an underlined word or phrase from the article. Following the sentence are three definitions. One definition is closest to the meaning of the underlined word. One definition is opposite or nearly opposite. Label those two definitions using the following key; do not label the remaining definition.

C—Closest   **O—Opposite or Nearly Opposite**

1. Writers have called it a "ghastly looking creature."

_____ a. attractive

_____ b. sleepy

_____ c. horrible

2. They wriggle like a "nest of serpents."

_____ a. make hissing sounds

_____ b. squirm

_____ c. remain motionless

3. In Denizens of the Deep, Frank Pullen said the giant creature "does not pursue his prey."

_____ a. run from

_____ b. chase

_____ c. select

4. There is no question that a giant squid is an awesome creature.

_____ a. impressive

_____ b. insignificant

_____ c. ignorant

5. One British scientist has called it "a <u>sluggish</u> animal."

_____ a. not very popular

_____ b. full of energy

_____ c. lacking alertness; slow to react

_____ Score 3 points for each correct C answer.

_____ Score 2 points for each correct O answer.

_____ **Total Score:** Using Words Precisely

Enter the four total scores in the spaces below, and add them together to find your Reading Comprehension Score. Then record your score on the graph on page 149.

Score	Question Type	Lesson 15
_____	Finding the Main Idea	
_____	Recalling Facts	
_____	Making Inferences	
_____	Using Words Precisely	
_____	**Reading Comprehension Score**	

Author's Approach

Put an X in the box next to the correct answer.

1. The main purpose of the first paragraph is to

☐ a. list various ways that others have described the giant squid.

☐ b. tell what H. G. Wells said about the giant squid.

☐ c. encourage readers to write their own descriptions of the giant squid.

2. What is the authors' purpose in writing "The Mystery of the Giant Squid"?

☐ a. to express an opinion about saving endangered animals

☐ b. to persuade readers to become ocean explorers

☐ c. to inform readers about the giant squid

3. From the statements below, choose those that you believe the authors would agree with.

☐ a. There is no good reason for people to study the giant squid.

☐ b. The giant squid may be one of the world's largest animals.

☐ c. It would be fascinating to find a live giant squid to study.

4. What do the authors imply by saying "No one has ever seen one [a giant squid] in its natural setting"?

☐ a. The giant squid is very shy and gentle.

☐ b. The giant squid lives in areas that people can't reach easily.

☐ c. The giant squid died out many years ago.

_____ Number of correct answers

Record your personal assessment of your work on the Critical Thinking Chart on page 150.

Summarizing and Paraphrasing

Follow the directions provided for question 1. Put an X in the box next to the correct answer for the other questions.

1. Complete the following one-sentence summary of the article using the lettered phrases from the phrase bank below. Write the letters on the lines.

Phrase Bank

a. scientific facts about the giant squid

b. stories of attacks by giant squids

c. descriptions of the giant squid

The article "The Mystery of the Giant Squid" begins with _____, goes on to explain _____, and ends with _____.

2. Below are summaries of the article. Choose the summary that says all the most important things about the article but in the fewest words.

☐ a. Even though most people have never seen a giant squid, alive or dead, many include it in their stories and books.

☐ b. The stories of sailors being attacked by giant squids may or may not be true. For example, the story of the *Brunswick* attack, in which a giant squid was cut up, cannot be proven. Either way, the giant squid is an interesting animal.

☐ c. Not much is known about the giant squid, but what we do know tells us that it is powerful and possibly dangerous. Encounters with the beast will teach us more about it.

3. Read the statement from the article below. Then read the paraphrase of that statement. Choose the reason that best tells why the paraphrase does not say the same thing as the statement.

Statement: We know a little about giant squids because now and then one is caught in a fishing net.

Paraphrase: We have learned about giant squids by studying the ones that have been caught in fishing nets or have washed up on shore.

☐ a. Paraphrase says too much.

☐ b. Paraphrase doesn't say enough.

☐ c. Paraphrase doesn't agree with the statement.

_____ Number of correct answers

Record your personal assessment of your work on the Critical Thinking Chart on page 150.

Critical Thinking

Follow the directions provided for questions 1, 2, and 3. Put an X in the box next to the correct answer for the other questions.

1. For each statement below, write *O* if it expresses an opinion or write *F* if it expresses a fact.

_____ a. The giant squid is one of the most frightening animals in the world.

_____ b. The giant squid found in Newfoundland in 1875 was 52 feet long.

_____ c. There is no need for anyone to fear the giant squid.

2. Using what you know about the octopus and what is told about giant squids in the article, name three ways the octopus is similar to and three ways the octopus is different from the giant squid. Cite the paragraph number(s) where you found details in the article to support your conclusions.

Similarities

_____

_____

Differences

_____

_____

3. Reread paragraph 13. Then choose from the letters below to correctly complete the following statement. Write the letters on the lines.

   According to paragraph 13, _____ happened because _____.

   a. the giant squid stopped attacking a boat near Newfoundland

   b. a sailor cut off the giant squid's arm

   c. some fishermen noticed a large object in the water

4. How is the giant squid an example of an angry animal?

   ☐ a. According to several stories, the giant squid attacks both ships and sailors without warning.

   ☐ b. The giant squid may reach a length of 75 feet and can weigh a ton.

   ☐ c. No one knows much about the giant squid.

5. What did you have to do to answer question 1?

   ☐ a. find a description (how something looks)

   ☐ b. find an opinion (what someone thinks about something)

   ☐ c. find a comparison (how things are the same)

_____ Number of correct answers

Record your personal assessment of your work on the Critical Thinking Chart on page 150.

Personal Response

Begin your own article about an imaginary encounter with a giant squid. _____

_____

_____

_____

_____

Self-Assessment

I can't really understand how _____

_____

_____

Compare and Contrast

Think about the articles you have read in Unit Three. Pick the three articles that tell about people who faced an animal with courage. Write the titles of the articles in the first column of the chart below. Use information you learned from the articles to fill in the empty boxes in the chart.

Title	What was the victim doing before the animal attack?	How did the victim fight or resist the attack?	What was the victim's condition after the attack?

Suppose you could interview one of the victims of the animal attack. Write two questions you would ask in your interview.

_____

_____

_____

Words-per-Minute Table

Unit Three

Directions: If you were timed while reading an article, refer to the Reading Time you recorded in the box at the end of the article. Use this Words-per-Minute Table to determine your reading speed for that article. Then plot your reading speed on the graph on page 148.

Lesson No. of Words	11 1,092	12 1,078	13 1,166	14 1,051	15 1,199	Seconds
1:30	728	719	777	701	799	90
1:40	655	647	700	631	719	100
1:50	596	588	636	573	654	110
2:00	546	539	583	526	600	120
2:10	504	498	538	485	553	130
2:20	468	462	500	450	514	140
2:30	437	431	466	420	480	150
2:40	410	404	437	394	450	160
2:50	385	380	412	371	423	170
3:00	364	359	389	350	400	180
3:10	345	340	368	332	379	190
3:20	328	323	350	315	360	200
3:30	312	308	333	300	343	210
3:40	298	294	318	287	327	220
3:50	285	281	304	274	313	230
4:00	273	270	292	263	300	240
4:10	262	259	280	252	288	250
4:20	252	249	269	243	277	260
4:30	243	240	259	234	266	270
4:40	234	231	250	225	257	280
4:50	226	223	241	217	248	290
5:00	218	216	233	210	240	300
5:10	211	209	226	203	232	310
5:20	205	202	219	197	225	320
5:30	199	196	212	701	218	330
5:40	193	190	206	185	212	340
5:50	187	185	200	180	206	350
6:00	182	180	194	175	200	360
6:10	177	175	189	170	194	370
6:20	172	170	184	631	189	380
6:30	168	166	179	162	184	390
6:40	164	162	175	158	180	400
6:50	160	158	171	154	175	410
7:00	156	154	167	150	171	420
7:10	152	150	163	147	167	430
7:20	149	147	159	143	164	440
7:30	146	144	155	140	160	450
7:40	142	141	152	137	156	460
7:50	139	138	149	134	153	470
8:00	137	135	146	131	150	480

Minutes and Seconds

Plotting Your Progress: Reading Speed

Unit Three

Directions: If you were timed while reading an article, write your words-per-minute rate for that article in the box under the number of the lesson. Then plot your reading speed on the graph by putting a small X on the line directly above the number of the lesson, across from the number of words per minute you read. As you mark your speed for each lesson, graph your progress by drawing a line to connect the X's.

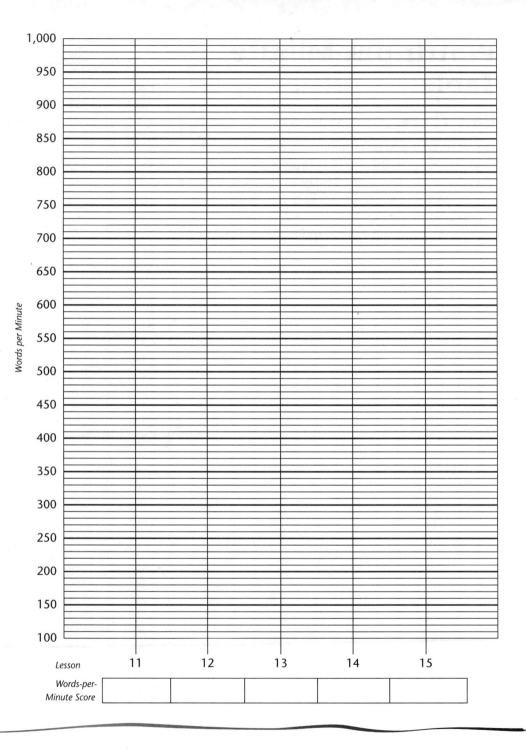

Lesson	11	12	13	14	15
Words-per-Minute Score					

Plotting Your Progress: Reading Comprehension

Unit Three

Directions: Write your Reading Comprehension Score for each lesson in the box under the number of the lesson. Then plot your score on the graph by putting a small X on the line directly above the number of the lesson and across from the score you earned. As you mark your score for each lesson, graph your progress by drawing a line to connect the X's.

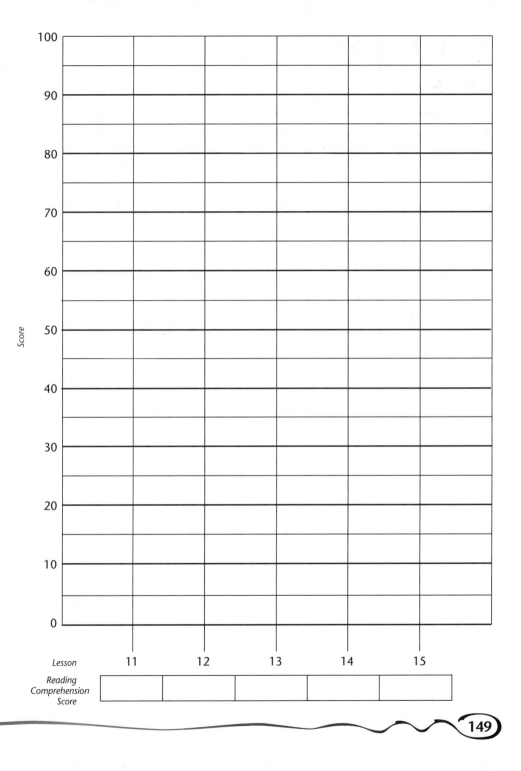

Plotting Your Progress: Critical Thinking

Unit Three

Directions: Work with your teacher to evaluate your responses to the Critical Thinking questions for each lesson. Then fill in the appropriate spaces in the chart below. For each lesson and each type of Critical Thinking question, do the following: Mark a minus sign (–) in the box to indicate areas in which you feel you could improve. Mark a plus sign (+) to indicate areas in which you feel you did well. Mark a minus-slash-plus sign (–/+) to indicate areas in which you had mixed success. Then write any comments you have about your performance, including ideas for improvement.

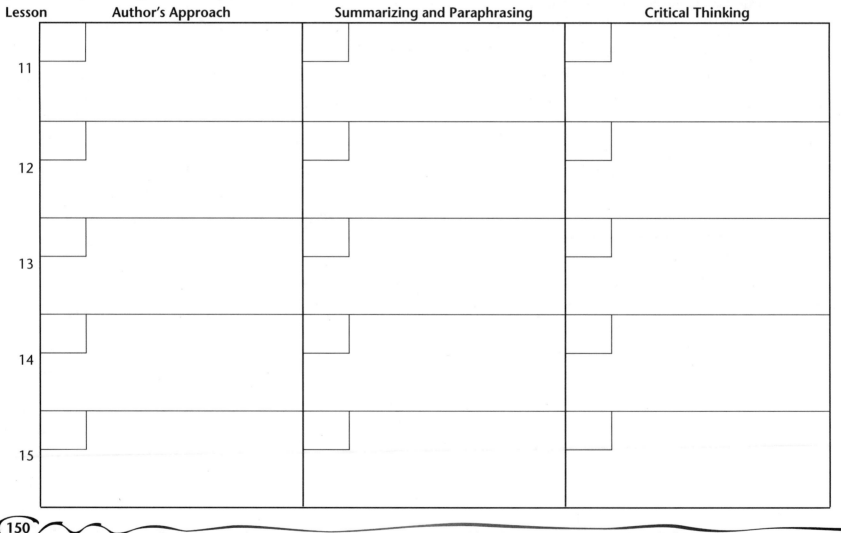

Lesson	Author's Approach	Summarizing and Paraphrasing	Critical Thinking
11			
12			
13			
14			
15			

Photo Credits